Unstoppable Joy

Unstoppable Joy

A Happier You in 12 Easy Steps

Ed Osworth
The Joy Professor

with

Jenifer Kay Hood

The purpose of this book is to educate and entertain. The authors and publisher shall have neither liability nor responsibility to any person or entity with respect to any loss or damage caused, or alleged to have been caused, directly or indirectly, by the information contained in this book. It is not intended as a substitute for proper medical care if the reader needs such.

Every effort has been made to make this text as complete and as accurate as possible. However, there may be mistakes, both typographical and in content. Therefore, this text should be used as a general guide and not as the ultimate source on any of the topics covered.

The examples used are not intended to represent or guarantee that anyone will achieve the same or similar results. Each individual's success depends on his or her background, dedication, desire and motivation.

Library of Congress Control Number: 2008932266

ISBN 10: 0-9817028-0-5

ISBN 13: 978-0-9817028-0-3

Published by Oregon Dreams Publishing LLC, Eugene Oregon

Design and layout by selfpublishing.com

Printed in the United States of America

CONTENTS

PREFACE

"Happiness depends upon ourselves."

--Aristotle

WANT to know exactly what lead you to this page? The reason you are here is because you had a desire in your mind for joy and peace in your life.

Your thirst for joy created a need. That need is what inspired me to write this book.

This book is specifically written for those looking for the quickest results with the least amount of philosophy and fluff.

The Universe lovingly guided me through a logical process that took me from stressed out misery to delightful joy. It hopefully blessed me with enough writing talent so, like Lewis and Clark, I could chart the path and pass it on to you.

To start with, I can describe the first part of my life as 45 miserable years. Then I discovered a technique that enabled me to create a new life. Since then I have experienced over 10 years of joy and ecstasy.

Not to brag, but I have more laughter, more fun and joyous feelings in the average day than many people have in a year. My mental and physical health is in a constant state of improvement because of this outlook. For example, since I shifted my perspective, I've lost over 80 pounds. But enough about me...

The process starts with uncovering the blockages that keep you from experiencing joy. The changes triggered by releasing those blockages are mind-boggling.

Folks who have learned this technique have seen radical improvements in health, both mental and physical. Some have experienced dramatic desired weight loss. I have listened to students who were at the end of their financial ropes gleefully explaining how they turned their fortunes around. I have rejoiced with those who related how they were so lonely and now have a companion. I have watched parents reopen lost communication with their children.

What triggered these dramatic changes? It was simply that these folks used the technique to rediscover the joy locked under self-destructive thinking patterns. They loosened up and let joy come to the surface. Once they started living in a state of joy their lives turned around and more and more bliss kept coming in.

How about you? Do you exist in joy? Do you look forward to every day as a joyous adventure? Do your family and your friends delight in your presence?

It's really not all that hard to have all of the above. The technique is not rocket science, that's for sure.

But a few words of warning:

First warning: some of this book is almost guaranteed to offend your sensibilities. I don't do fluff and I don't tiptoe around truths that may disturb you. There are lots of other books out there that will spend tens, if not hundreds, of pages gently and non-offensively revealing to you the intricacies and subtleties behind even one of these 12 steps.

I am very blunt, irreverent and to the point. When something works – I tell you. I do my best to explain why in simple English. You can spend 50 years researching, debating and meditating on it or you can save a lot of time and simply try it.

If the shoe fits… wear it!

Want to try a one of the simpler steps right this minute and prove it to yourself?

Great, go to page 92 and read: *STEP 7: HOW TO GROW APPRECIATION AND JOY FEEDBACK LOOPS*

Give it a try and keep in mind it is just a tiny part of this book. If one technique doesn't work or is too uncomfortable – try another step. They all lead in the same direction.

Second warning: it's not usually an instantaneous change. It may take some time to retrain your brain. After all, you didn't instantly program your mind to see things the way you're seeing them now. It took decades to train your mind to hide the joy living within you.

The good news is, when you use the techniques in *Unstoppable Joy*, it won't take you nearly as long to retrain your mind for a life of happiness. Some folks can do it as little as a month.

The rate of progress is directly related to the amount of desire you have for joy.

The reason this transformation can happen so fast is that once you have tasted the delicious nectar of joyous living there is no turning back.

So, are you ready to free your "Unstoppable Joy" from the cramped quarters of self-doubt and judgment inside you?

When it finally runs free you will wonder why you ever kept it in a cage.

What will you need to accomplish this?

Well, you will not need any religion. The system I teach should harmonize perfectly with most religious teachings, although my personal opinions may not.

You will not need to meditate for hours or lie in a bed of nails. You probably won't need to go through hours of expensive therapy to apply this method. Nor will you need to fast or to endlessly repeat positive mantras to yourself.

All you're really going to need is a willingness to look at the way you have programmed your mind to "see" the world. Then you will have to decide for yourself if the way you're presently looking at the world is serving your best interest.

If your old habits are no longer serving your best interest then I will give you precise instructions on how to change your life to a life of *Unstoppable Joy.*

ACKNOWLEDGMENTS

LISTING all of those who have benefited me and helped in the creation of this book with their unconditional love, support and encouragement could fill a book on its own so I will keep this as short as possible.

First and foremost I must give proper credit to my co-author and life long friend Jenifer Hood. Without her gentle but firm encouragement and superb editing skills this book might never have made it out of my brain.

Thanks to all of the following in no particular order:

Kerry Lynn for lighting my path for so many years. Violet for opening the final door. Kitty Starr Stephens who is always available as a practical sounding board. Judith Elliott for opening me to the way of Zen. Robin MoonRaven for proving to me that miracles never stop. Ella Crow for showing me the dark side of the power of my words. Cherie Gypsy Dancer for showing me new paths to the same goal. Bijan for walking the walk and Will Linville for his unique encouragement. My brother Joseph for showing me how far creativity can reach and brother John for telling me an unfortunate truth that saved my life. My sisters: Kate for being an invisible angel; and Barbara for always believing in me. Ken McCarthy for showing me the true key to success is generosity and caring. Jeff and Bryan Eisenberg for limitless inspiration. Roy Williams for giving my brain something new to chew on every week. Larry Crane for showing me the simple solution is the best solution. Jerry and Esther Hicks for proving to me that I was not completely crazy. *The Course in Miracles* for validating what I knew inside all of my life. All those merciless nuns in Catholic school who insisted I learn the English language inside out and backwards for creating the mind of a writer.

All the folks who read and/or purchased this book or my previous writings for supporting me spiritually, intellectually and financially. The

United States of America for being a place where a person as crazy as me can publish a book.

And Elyse Hope Killoran, John Assaraf, Colleen Benelli, Steve Murray, Gary Renard, Doreen Virtue, Catherine Ponder, Louis Hay, John Gray, Paul Scheele, Hale Dwoskin, Deepak Chopra, Michael Port, Dan Poynter, Dan Kennedy, Miguel Ruiz, Eckhart Tolle, Brenda Ueland, Elsom Eldridge, Aaron Shepard, Jane Roberts, Robert Middleton, Dr. Michael Norwood, Joe Vitale, Elisa Olalde, Clayton Makepeace, Jack Canfield, Marianne Williamson, Stephen Covey, Dr. Alex Loyd, Stephen Pierce, Valerie Jayne, Tim Cooney, Robert Ringer, Anjuli Sutara, Brian Tracy, Marci Shimoff, Lisa Nichols, Bob Proctor, James Ray, Bill Harris, John Assaraf, Harv Eker, Mark Hasting, Marianne Williamson, Penelope Russianoff, Brian Rogers, Gaylin Howard, Laura Biggs, Pascal Chapelle, Alexandria Brown, Dr Ken Evoy, Phil Wiley, Simona Tozier, Yanik Silver, Jim Edwards, Neale Donald Walsch, Denny Hatch, Kevin Wood, Sue Supriano, Siva, Elvy Mussika, Nancy Venuti, Christian Peritore, Steve Gurzi, Rose Sanez, Fred Gleek, Mark Hasting, Randy Woodruff, Jeff Bode, Kimberly Cooney, Hal Twigg, Gabi Tolens, Lonnie and Owl Sloan, Kenneth Pierce, Randy Newman, Dr John Miner, Mike Mikel, Laird Funk, Randy Pausch, Kathy DiDonato, George Cappony, Cory Rudl, Terry Dean, Karen Petersen, Susan Taylor and Rodger Peterson,

Dedication: This book is dedicated to Anita and John, my wonderful and loving parents, for far too many things to mention. No finer folks ever walked this planet.

CHAPTER 1

WHY YOU DESERVE A LIFE OF JOY AND HAPPINESS

"If I can't be sorry then, I might as well be glad."

--Edna St. Vincent Millay

MANY feel that they don't even deserve a life of happiness, much less *Unstoppable Joy*. What nonsense.

No one deserves it more than you.

Why do you deserve it?

Because of who you are.

To start, you're the most uniquely interesting person who ever existed in the history of humankind.

You are the best "you" that ever lived. No one else is like you. You are 100% unique to this universe.

And there will never, ever, be another you.

You are an integral part of the most sophisticated and powerful system ever imagined or created. That system is the universe we live in.

The universe doesn't create spare parts. It may create parts that look slightly alike, but even an identical twin is a unique force in this universe. So you are absolutely necessary and 100% unmatched by any human being.

You are not only necessary, but you are contributing in some way to the continued existence and evolution of the universe. Just as every cell in our body is necessary for our existence, every life form in the universe has a part to play in its existence.

Everything you do in this lifetime effects people not only right around you, but people you aren't even remotely aware of. The way you live and the actions you do affect not only the present but the future as well.

So, in truth, you are a very important human being.

And, given that you are an important and powerful part of this universe, everyone's world would be better if you were in joy virtually all the time.

That's right. Joy. Not uncertainty. Not fear. Not worry. Not sadness. Joy.

You should be waking up with a smile on your face and a song in your heart. If you went about joyfully fulfilling your destiny and contributing your unique talents and perspectives back to the universe, you would be serving others in a way that would be contagious to those around you. I'm talking about creating so much joy that even the hardest of life challenges would be easy to overcome.

You were born to be in joy. When you were an infant you actually were in joy almost all of the time.

You came here completely innocent and joyous with a unique destiny for you alone to fulfill. You were absolutely delighted to have a chance to participate and play on this planet and share your joy and laughter with your fellow human beings.

But for most of us, something happened along the way to adulthood that took a lot of joyousness away.

Here's proof.

According to a recent study by Drs. Gael Crystal & Patrick Flanagan, adults laugh roughly 15 times per day, while children laugh upwards of 400 times a day!

I would say laughter is a pretty good indicator of joy. If children laugh over 400 times a day and adults laugh 15, I think we lost something very important along the way.

Joy. And with it, better health.

Laughter offers many important health benefits. "People become healthier from laughter," explains Judy Goldblum-Carlton, a humor therapist for Children's Division of Pediatric Hematology/Oncology at the University of Maryland Hospital. "It improves circulation. When you laugh heartily, every organ is being massaged including your heart, lungs and digestive system. Headaches can just go away. When you laugh the endorphins released make you feel this elation. It makes those big decisions seem so much less important."

How good is joy and laughter for us?

Another study of folks watching funny movies versus horror movies showed that with laughter, blood flow increased 22%, while under stress it decreased 35%

And, according to a study by John Assaraf, people who are happy earn $750,000+ more in their lifetime than unhappy people.

If there is no question that it is good for our mental, physical and financial health for us to laugh often, why don't we do it nearly as much as when we are young?

The reason is that something huge got lost along the path to adulthood. For most of us that something is the wondrous state that comes so naturally to children.

You probably would agree that if you still laughed 400 times a day and looked at life as a thing of wonder, every day would seem much different.

Not only is it possible to live in such bliss, it is our natural state. Somehow things got twisted around so we started believing joyousness was supposed to be an occasional pleasure, rather than a way of life.

Yet it is our right to exist in joy every day of our life. It is in our best interest to exist in joy. It is in the best interest of all those around us when we relate to them in a state of joy. Not to mention that it is more fun to be in a state of joy.

For hundreds of years medical science has known happier people are healthier people. Personnel professionals will tell you those who keep a positive attitude have better work performance. Having a sunny disposition is even good for your personal relationships.

We all instinctively know that it feels better to be in joy than it does to be in anger or fear. I have never met a person who does not feel better when they are in a state of joy.

As my friends, acquaintances and business partners will tell you: yours truly is in a state of joy virtually all the time. I am known as "Joyful Ed" near and far.

Is the world I live in any different than yours? Logic tells you that it can't be. I have to be in the same reality as you. There is no other choice, correct?

Perhaps. But consider this: I suspect that the world you see looks a lot different from mine.

Why? Because every single day I see this world as a delightful place. I make friends easily and live a relatively care free life. People treat me fantastically.

I see beauty all around me and because of that I am constantly enjoying exactly where I am. Oh, yes, and I laugh several hundred times a day.

Am I in some sort of delusion?

I think that's a perfectly legitimate question for you to be asking.

Is it delusional to see this life we live as a precious gift and this place we live as a wonderful and embracing planet?

That's a decision you're going to have to make on your own....

But before you do, finish reading this book.

You may be surprised by what you have been accepting as a "normal" view of life. You may be shocked at how much of that viewpoint has been manipulated by those who did not have your best interests in mind.

Personally, I think it's delusional to see life the way 99% of people on this planet do: As a place full of struggle, fear, worry, and stress.

I will offer you plenty of evidence for you to consider about the way you have trained yourself to filter your perception of the world. Hopefully the majority of what I offer you to consider will be things you may have never pondered before.

All of my life I have been a skeptic myself, so it is easy for me to imagine how skeptical you are right now.

My purpose in writing this book is not to ask you to have faith that what I am saying is true or even that it will work for you.

All I am asking is that you give serious consideration to the concepts I am going to present to you. If you feel they are valid then give the suggestions a try. If they work for you, you'll know it in a very short period of time.

If they work at all for you, I bet there is no way you would ever consider turning back.

Enter into this with as much skepticism as you like.

But at the same time be sure to retain a grain of skepticism about the logic behind the thinking processes you have accumulated up to this point in your life.

I have chosen Joy as more than an attitude. For me it is a lifestyle I will share with the entire world.

How about you?

Are you ready to free your *Unstoppable Joy*?

CHAPTER 2

WHERE DID YOUR JOY GO?

A child of five would understand this. Send someone to fetch a child of five.

-- Groucho Marx

I read somewhere once that there was a point in my life when I was completely joyous about everything in my world. Sure, there was the issue of needing a change and being hungry, but otherwise I felt loved and admired by nearly everyone I came in contact with.

Like me, you probably don't remember this sense of unbridled joy, because back in those days you didn't have words for what you were experiencing. So you gurgled and shrieked and giggled and made up sounds that tried to convey your sense of delight. Unfortunately, no one could understand you.

But joyous you were. Most likely your parents beamed with pride as you tried to explain the wonders you were discovering in the incredible world around you. You rambled on in your private language but your parents, grandparents and even strangers in the supermarket knew how delighted you were to be alive.

So the question is, what happened? Where did that joy go?

As an infant you believed you were loved and that everyone around you had your best interests at heart.

If you saw something you wanted you simply went for it. You never asked yourself, "Do I deserve this? Is it okay for me to have this? What happens if I reach for it and fall from my high chair?"

No, you simply thought, "That cookie looks good. It is probably delicious and will bring me joy." So you crawled, reached, cried, and did anything you could to get that cookie. If you weren't able to get your parents' attention, the family dog could easily distract you. If you never got the cookie that was okay because by the time you awoke from your nap you no longer remembered the cookie. You simply went forward in life.

Isn't it amazing that you didn't need any self-confidence to do those things? The reason you don't is because you're not even aware of yourself as a separate being. You are one with everyone because you believe that everyone is there to act in your best interest.

Even though society didn't measure your intelligence as especially potent or your ability to reason as developed, you had a level of confidence that allowed you to remain joyous regardless of what people thought of you. Whether one attributes that freedom to lack of experience or lack of cynicism, the end result was simply that people adored your ability to enjoy life and embrace whatever came.

But as the years went by you were taught that sometimes your desires would conflict with those of others. You stopped being welcomed into your parents' bedroom; your grandparents wanted you to be able to use the toilet by yourself; your mother exchanged her breast for a smelly plastic bottle; and your teachers required you to sit still and speak when spoken to. By then your entire worldview had been turned around. The party was over.

In those first five years you lived a life of incredible joy, boundless freedom and marvelous experience as you gazed at the world from your distinctive point of view. Everything from the clouds in the sky to the gooey ooze of a snail on the ground was incredibly interesting and fascinating.

It would have been so delightful to talk about all of those things in school without having to raise your hand or wait your turn. But, unfortunately, the educational system is not designed for you to share your impressions of the universe. It is designed to teach you someone else's.

Very quickly you are taught that your joy, delight, knowledge, opinions and even your tastes are pretty much of zero value to society at large.

By ignoring the free and joyous person you were, society declared your delightful inner world null and void. To your teachers, your parents, and your peers you simply were an empty vessel they could fill with whatever they considered worth knowing. No more bursting out with joy when you saw the first flowers of spring. No more singing unless you could sing on key. Joy became reserved for special occasions and you soon forgot that every day is special.

On top of that, you started learning about all of the things you needed to worry about and fear.

Soon thereafter you learned that acceptance from the group depended on polishing the social skills of gossiping, criticizing and complaining, instead of how to enjoy the moment.

You learned Murphy's Law, Catch-22 and what the word "snafu" originally meant.

Then you are told you will have to struggle and suffer for the majority of your life in order to achieve an amorphous thing labeled "success."

As Jane Nelson puts it, "Where did we get the crazy idea that in order to make children do better, first we have to make them feel worse? Think of the last time you felt humiliated or treated unfairly. Did you feel like cooperating or doing better?"

Yet so it goes. By the time you're a teenager you have a profound case of Joy Amnesia. You can't remember your joyous infancy, those flashes of delight you still found when you were six, or even how to trust yourself, let alone anyone else.

How sad that is.

CHAPTER 3

HOW BEING IN JOY CHANGES EVERYTHING

Change and growth take place when a person has risked himself and dares to become involved with experimenting with his own life.

~ Herbert Otto

HOW important is joy if you want to manifest success, love and money?

In a nutshell, it is the most important factor. Why? Because joy is the foundation of all of the above and more.

Don't believe me? There is evidence all around you.

Take a look at the videos of any of the dozens of trainers who teach how to manifest prosperity and live a better life. Instead of listening to what they say, look at their attitudes, look in their faces, especially the eyes.

Bob Proctor, Joe Vitale, Esther Hicks, Dennis Waitley, John Assaraf, James Ray, Eckhart Tolle, Joseph Campbell, Caroline Myss, Gary Zukav, Abraham-Hicks, Marianne Williamson, Deepak Chopra, Neale Donald Walsch, Byron Katie, Gregg Braden, and Debbie Ford all have one thing in common.

They are very joyous people. You can see it in everything they do. You can see it in their eyes; you can hear it in the way they present things.

Now look beyond the motivational and self-improvement people:

Wayne Dyer, for example. Look at Oprah Winfrey and other entertainers that you admire. Look at the people you consider role models.

Instead of looking at the details and mechanics of what it is they do, look at the attitude they put out to the world. I would be willing to bet that 99% of the time you're going to find a joyous attitude.

Now I have a question for you. Which came first, the chicken or the egg?

Did they become joyous because they became successful and rose to the top? Or did they become successful and rise to the top because they were joyous?

In virtually every case you'll find they were positive, joyous and can do people before they became rich and successful.

Joy is not the goal at the end of the path. Joy is the path.

You'll hear that more than once in this book because it is core to understanding how joy works to build a prosperous and more fulfilled life.

Joy is the path.

Joy must come first. Every ability to manifest, all of the good intentions, the charitable deeds and even all the gold in Fort Knox won't create a fulfilling life without the magic ingredient of joy.

Once you bring that magic ingredient into your life everything else you want in life naturally follows.

There is something else for you to consider. Something that was a huge motivator for me to transform my life into one of constant joy...

That is the indisputable fact that joy equals freedom.

Freedom from worry. Freedom from anger. Freedom from feeling apprehensive about life. Freedom from the suffocating chains of judging others. Freedom from having to be serious.

Most importantly, it is freedom from concerning yourself about what others think of you.

But those are just a few of the "freedom froms." It's the many "freedom tos" that are really incredible.

Freedom to be wildly creative. Freedom to laugh and play. Freedom to make others laugh and feel joyous. Freedom to be kind and generous in every situation. Freedom to smile all of the time. Freedom to know that the joy you feel now is the joy you will feel always.

Freedom to live every single day as the joyous, exciting, fulfilling adventure that it really is.

Once you have tasted this freedom you will never, ever be able to go back to your self-imposed prison again.

Chapter 4

Why Joy Is Always In Your Best Interest

Everyday we are engaged in a miracle we don't even recognize; the blue sky, white clouds, green leaves, the black, curious eyes of a child—our own two eyes. All is a miracle.

--Thich Nhat Hanh

Is it in your best interest to look at life as a continual battle where the slightest little error on your part can cause an unlimited amount of pain and suffering? To see the world full of horrible people who are out to get you? To concentrate on all of the imperfection, all of the dirt, all the scabs, all of the garbage you see around you?

Or is it in your best interest to see life as a marvelous and delightful gift? To see the world as a wondrous place full of beautiful and friendly people? To concentrate on all of the beauty that surrounds you and can easily be seen in every direction?

In truth, the world doesn't care how you look at it. The world you see outside yourself is completely objective. What we call reality has no viewpoint. The world and the circumstances in your life simply are.

The way that things and circumstances affect you is entirely controlled by your viewpoint.

Have you ever thought about it like that?

I can hear many of you readers screaming, "This is unrealistic. You are telling us to deny looking at reality and seeing what is there."

That is not what I am asking at all. I am asking you to make a more informed decision about which parts of reality you allow to enter your mind and occupy your thoughts.

What is your definition of reality?

Is reality what a scientist says it is? Is reality what a minister says it is? Is reality what the teachers say it is? Is reality what the news says it is?

I think you may agree that in fact the most important reality in the universe is what you perceive from your particular vantage point. And you have a much bigger part in what you perceive than you may well realize.

It is a well-known fact that no two people see things in exactly the same way. As a matter of fact, there's really no way to prove that any two people see anything exactly the same way.

Which means that the same things that make one person miserable could quite likely make another person happy. Good examples are masochists. They enjoy pain.

A masochist has figured out a certain perspective on pain that allows him or her to receive enjoyment from it. Masochists control their perspective on pain.

Now if one person can control his perspective so that he receives pleasure when another inflicts pain on him, do you think maybe you could change your perspective enough so that if somebody cuts you off in traffic or delays your shopping progress by a few minutes it wouldn't bother you?

We are taught how to control everything else in life *but* our viewpoint of the world. Yet it is completely within our best interest to control our viewpoint of the world.

Think about it.

Does it serve your best to go through life in fear or anger? Or does it serve you best to go through life in joy?

Never forget it is your decision. It has nothing to do with what the outside world is allegedly doing to you.

It really is a matter of self-interest. You are the one who has to live this life in this body, no one else. How do you want to see every day? How do you want to feel when you wake up? And how do you want to feel when you go to sleep?

Personally I spent decades going through life in fear and stress. Not once did I question whether those states of mind served my best interest. I just thought that was how life was supposed to be: hell.

Since I switched my perspective to a life of joy I am absolutely sure this perspective serves my best interest. I am happier. I am healthier. I am more focused. I wake up every morning with a smile on my face anxious to get involved with a new day of joyous adventures.

I have made my choice to see life from a joyful perspective. And I give everyone else the freedom of seeing life through whatever perspective they decide is in their best interest.

The bottom line: Joy is a choice.

I know that may sound totally crazy to you right now. But read on and you will see why this is true.

Chapter 5

It is Easier to Change Your Mind than to Change the World

Happiness does not depend on outward things, but on the way we see them.

~ Leo Tolstoy

HOW can joy, much less *Unstoppable Joy*, be possible in this crazy and mixed up world?

The beauty of the answer lies in its simplicity.

It doesn't have to do with how wealthy you are. It doesn't have to do with how powerful you are. It doesn't have to do with how healthy you are. It doesn't even have to do with how intelligent, successful, spiritual or holy you are.

It has to do with something far more important than all of those factors.

The difference between folks who struggle in lives of "quiet desperation" and those enjoy a consistently joyous and a successful life has nothing to do with the world one lives in.

It has to do with how one sees the world. To live in a joyous world you first must change the way you look at it.

If attaining joy was dependent upon the outside circumstances in your life I'm afraid it would be an impossible goal.

Whether you're the gal or guy who sleeps under the freeway off ramp or whether you're Oprah or Donald Trump, life is going to present you with an endless supply of challenges and lessons.

Here is the reason why most people cannot attain a consistent state of joy.

They believe that joy is a goal to be attained.

They feel that if outside circumstances were just a little bit different they would be completely joyous. If they could only change a few things in their personal reality then they could feel the joy they want so badly.

Unfortunately, that is putting the cart in front of the horse. First comes joy, then comes the solution to our life challenges.

It's not our fault that we believe we must first experience suffering and sacrifice and then the joy will come. We were taught to feel exactly that way for most of our lives. People we trusted told us joy is something that comes after we have changed the outside world enough to allow all the things we want in our lives to appear.

Some of that programming was inadvertent, and some was deliberate.

One reason we were programmed this way is that a desire to purchase new stuff fuels a consumer-oriented society like ours. If one can confuse people into thinking that joy will come when they have bought the right amount of things it is a very effective way to sell.

Those who would like to sell us their products will supply us with a constant barrage of new things to want. And they would love for you to believe that you will be joyous once you acquire all of these things.

I lived my life under that premise for close to 45 years. I acquired all sorts of status possessions. I drove a Mercedes and a new Cadillac, ate in the best restaurants, vacationed where I liked, won lots of awards and competed successfully against the best in my business.

But there was something missing. I wasn't exactly sure what it was at the time but I knew there was a big piece missing. Actually, the more successful I became the more obvious it was that something wasn't there.

There was very little joy in my life. In a way I was like a man in an ocean of abundance with hardly any drinking water. Although I had plenty of stuff on the outside, inside I had very little of what was important. Joy.

Then I had some problems with my real estate business, lost all my toys and luxuries and ended up in bankruptcy court. Since I didn't have joy before I went bankrupt, you can imagine how I felt going through it.

To make things worse, at the same time as the bankruptcy, my marriage of 25 years fell apart. My life partner was leaving me for good.

I felt lower than a dead skunk tossed down a well. I reached a crisis point.

I became grossly overweight and unhealthy. I got so depressed I couldn't see any way out of it. I really felt like life was no longer worth living.

I even entertained ways of leaving this life.

My lowest point was on a dreary Christmas Eve. I had just finished the bankruptcy proceedings.

In my mind was a constant chorus of voices, reinforcing how miserable I felt. It was beyond failure. It was a disaster.

On that night I sat in my very used Kia in the parking lot of a drugstore in Grants Pass. There were Christmas lights all around. My soon to be ex-wife had just gone in to buy some wrapping paper. I didn't go in with her. I could've cared less if it was Christmas Eve.

Rain was pouring down in buckets. Even the weather seemed to reflect my mood.

My mind was so black it was like I was peering through a pinhole at the outside world.

A mother and child walked by. She looked over, gave me a big smile and said, "Merry Christmas."

I certainly hope she didn't hear my response.

Hidden behind the anonymous foggy glass on the windshield of that beat up Kia I screamed back. "Shut up! I *hate* Christmas."

And I kept screaming through the tears pouring from my eyes. "I hate Christmas. I hate my marriage. I hate my life. Most of all I hate this asshole that I have become."

I peered through the mist and found I was lucky. They hadn't seen me or heard what I said. But I certainly had.

As I mentally reviewed the horror of the words I said it made me sick to my very soul.

All my life I had pushed and pushed. I had worked so hard and made so many sacrifices. I'd moved mountains to assure my success. I played all the games.

And here I was crying like a baby. Feeling like there was nothing to look forward to, only more misery and stress.

That very moment I received guidance from a most startling and unexpected source. That loving mother's wonderful greeting was a catalyst to help me see how far from my joyful beginnings I had traveled. Over the next few years I was guided on a path that led from abject misery to joy beyond my wildest imagination.

I can no longer even recognize the person I was 10 years ago on that dreary Christmas Eve. The gift I was given by having this path revealed to me has opened me up to an entirely new world.

But the gift did come with a price...

The price was that it must be shared with as many people as possible.

So that, my friends, is why you are reading this book.

The process that was revealed to me for finding joy is both very simple and incredibly complex. That sounds contradictory I know. But whereas the path is simple, changing your outlook will go against almost everything you know as logical and common sense.

This is because the vast majority of people in our society are looking at the world through a very warped perspective of fear. This fear permeates everything from the news, television, radio, magazines, to our daily chats around the office.

Everywhere you look you see messages or people who are telling you that all sorts of horrible things can happen to you. Terrorists can blow you up. Horrible diseases can catch you in an instant and turn your life to misery. Friends can turn on you and murder you. Your priest might molest your children. Thieves will steal your identity or your possessions. A nice guy in a cubicle near yours may march in with an automatic weapon and do who knows what. Global warming. Famine. Hurricanes. Fires. And on and on and on...

Do all of these things happen? Yes. Are they likely to happen to you? Not really. And a universal truth in life is focusing your attention on any of them is not going to make them any less likely to happen.

In our society, this viewpoint of fear is so pervasive that it seems as if looking at life any other way is crazy.

So here are two definitions I want to share with you before we go any further:

Mass Consciousness: It consists of the thousands of common shared perceptions in society based on the assumption that life is mostly dangerous and hostile. An obvious example is Murphy's Law. Mass Consciousness certainly isn't in your best interest.

The Fear Paradox: Webster's defines a paradox as, "a statement that is seemingly contradictory or opposed to common sense and yet is perhaps true." While most folk believe they can avoid fearful and dangerous circumstances by focusing on them, the Fear Paradox is that when you focus on the things you fear you attract those negative events.

Franklin Delano Roosevelt said it best, "We have nothing to fear but fear itself!"

Murphy's Law states, "Whatever can go wrong will go wrong."

Murphy's smarter brother realized, "Whatever can go right, will go right."

Guess which Murphy had a happier life?

CHAPTER 6

THE LAW OF PERCEPTION

We don't live in a world of reality, we live in a world of perceptions.

~ Gerald J. Simmons

THESE days there's a lot of talk about the Law of Attraction. But the most effective way to get what you want in your life has more to do with the Law of Perception.

The Law of Perception is quite simple and is the basis for turning your perspective around. It is also the basis my "Joy Technique," an advanced training program to jump start folks into a life of complete joy.

Here it is.

"Your internal dialogs dictate what you will see and experience in your outside reality"

Although the law itself is simple, its implications are staggering.

Out of all the thousands of things they teach you in school they don't teach you very much about the voices that are going on in your mind and how they are affecting everything you perceive.

Yet those voices are one of the most noticeable things in our lives.

Constantly jabbering away and commenting on—and in most cases criticizing—almost everything we see around us.

And I say voices because there's more than one. There is usually a loud and critical voice in the foreground but there is also a gentler more loving voice in the background.

Since time immemorial great writers have written about the conflict between those two voices. This battle is so much a part of being human that it is often humorously depicted as an angel on one shoulder and a devil on the other. Which isn't to say this is a question of religion but rather a contrast between the original consciousness of you and the person you became after years of programming.

In this book you're going to learn how to identify each of those voices and use that knowledge to your advantage.

Because once you can control those internal dialogs you will have far more control over what you see and experience in your world.

Those voices both have significantly more power then you ever imagined. By learning to control them you can mold your life into a new shape—if that is your desire.

Applying the truth of the Law of Perception and controlling those internal dialogs can change the entire world you are seeing. You have way more control over what you perceive then you realize.

The Law of Perception may seem so totally alien to your "reality" that you are snickering right now.

It certainly did to mine. Until I proved it works.

The Law of Perception is based on timeless truths that have been taught by for thousands of years by wise men and women and enlightened Avatars.

It is also based on the latest scientific discoveries in quantum physics.

Basically, what keeps us locked in a world of stress, strife, disease, problems and confusion is our thinking patterns. We have taught ourselves to believe everything we see is "reality," and therefore is fixed and unchangeable.

If reality is fixed and unchangeable you can feel pretty hopeless. This would mean your entire existence is just like a ping-pong ball being bounced around by random events. That sort of worldview can put you in a state of mind where you feel a victim. And it's the way the vast majority of people see their life.

Thank goodness it really isn't the truth at all.

The reasons we have been programmed into this worldview are quite complex. In a nutshell, we have been taught things are a certain way so we can be controlled and manipulated.

But I hear you saying, "Science proves that reality is fixed and unchangeable, right?"

Nope, actually many respected names in science believe just the opposite. Our own individual reality is based more on what we "perceive" is out there, rather than what is actually there.

Testing with PET (Positron Emission Tomography) scans and Functional MRI (Magnetic Resonance Imaging) scans clearly demonstrate that the same part of your brain lights up whether you're looking at something, imagining something, or just remembering it.

This means that your thoughts have a huge influence on your perception of the world.

So, as far as perception goes, we are not victims at all: just the opposite.

We control what we perceive. The external influences do not control what we perceive.

Consider this: at any one moment in time you are surrounded by approximately four million sensory inputs that you can choose to focus on. Yep, believe it or not, that is what science has measured.

Seem like an exaggeration?

Look around. You can choose from every 1/10 inch of your desk, every pencil, every piece of shag on your carpet. Pull out a magnifier and you can multiply the choices even farther. Thousands of sights, smells, sounds, and sensations that can be interpreted as warm, cold, soft, sharp, bright, dull, near, far, and the list goes on and on...ad infinitum.

Here is the kicker. We got 4,000,000 to choose from but, surprise, science has shown the brain can only experience 2,000 at a time!

So what about the other 3,998,000?

Well, we *choose* not to let those in through our filters.

And what are those filters? They are your belief systems!

See where I am going here?

We filter out the vast majority of the sensory data that surrounds us. And because each of us filters out different stuff, it stands to reason that each individual person's reality is not exactly the same.

So the secret to existing in joy has a whole lot to do with deciding which of those filters you are going to use to sort out the vast amounts of sensory data around you.

Simple example. You are driving down the highway. There is a car up ahead on the right, pulled over by a police officer. On the left, there is a gorgeous sunset over a beautiful pond full of geese.

Which do you choose as you drive by? Where do you look: the beauty or the stress? It is always your choice. The guy who is pulled over has no more or less to do with your life than the beautiful sight.

Another simple example...

You are in line in a store. There are some magazines in the rack in front of you and you scan the headlines. At the front of the line are an extremely slow checker and a customer who has forgotten her checkbook. Do you relax and pick up a magazine; or do you get irritated and impatient with the situation?

It is always your choice.

Your day is full of literally thousands of small decisions that are equivalent to those examples. Thousands of times you can choose the beauty of the moment or the stress you create by wishing things were different.

A big part of grounding oneself in joy is realizing this simple, obvious fact and using it to your advantage by training your mind to choose the beauty.

I don't want you to take my word for it. No, not at all.

You will learn the one of the greatest lessons possible by proving it yourself –not through another's second hand experience.

That lesson is basically this: The images and internal dialogs in your mind are major controlling factors in your perception of reality.

All of our lives we have been told that what you can see with your own eyes is reality.

What I didn't get to discover until I was nearly 50 was that we get to control what we see.

Once we master how to control what we see (in other words what we let through our filtration system) we can literally change the world around us (our reality) and exist in a state of joy.

Those images and internal dialogs are literally creating the reality you are experiencing this very moment. Change those dialogs and you will change your world.

You will learn this empowering truth by tasting the delicious fruits of joy for yourself.

Your own experience will show you how unbelievably important and powerful those images and internal dialogs are. Then you will know how powerful your mind is.

Once you discover this, you will realize how much of your mind's power you were inadvertently using to shoot yourself in the foot. You will recognize thoughts that do not serve your best interests when they start appearing.

You will learn how to control what your mind sees, says and does in such a way as to be able to use your mind to consistently receive what you really desire.

Soon each day will reflect a continuous feedback loop of joyful existence.

And why? Because you simply made the decision to take charge of your point of view by using the Law of Perception.

That is how simple the *Unstoppable Joy* way is.

Fast. Easy. Fun.

CHAPTER 7

WHAT IS A BELIEF SYSTEM?

A man must not swallow more beliefs than he can digest.

--Havelock Ellis

THROUGHOUT this book you're going to hear me use a term that might be familiar to you but which you may not fully understand. That term is belief system.

At its most basic level a belief system is anything one believes and accepts as fact without experiencing it personally.

Our minds are full of belief systems. Some of these belief systems are quite helpful as they prevent us from doing things that would harm us. An example is the belief system that if you walk in front of a car you are going to get seriously injured. There is no need for anyone to experience walking in front of a car to find out how painful it would be.

However, in most cases the belief systems the one carries have very little to do with reality or fact. Most of them simply consist of things we were told or taught and accepted as fact without question.

When I was young we were taught that if one sat in front of a draft one would catch a cold. It was a commonly held belief ascribed to by nearly every set of parents I knew. And, interestingly, children who grew up with that belief system would catch colds if they sat in front of a draft.

Eventually that "belief system" was proved to be completely false.

Sitting in front of draft had nothing to do getting colds. So a new belief system replaced that belief system.

And that is the pattern with most belief systems. They get replaced with new ones.

Originally, scientists believed that the stars and planets revolved around the earth. This was replaced by a different belief system that the earth revolved around the sun. For a large chunk of our history people thought that the earth was flat. This was replaced by a belief system that the earth is round.

Belief systems constantly evolve and change. In a short span of 60 years the definition of the smallest particle of matter has changed and changed again, shaping and reshaping the entire scientific belief system.

And think of how our medical and social belief systems have altered over the past 40 years! When I was in my twenties the five-minute mile was broken and today it is routine for someone to run a mile in under four-minutes. Living memory attests to the bigotry of Jim Crow laws and now a woman or an African-American can aspire to be president of the United States. At one time the USDA's Food Pyramid told us the absolute best foods to eat were eggs, meats, butter, whole milk, and lots of potatoes. I remember how everyone laughed when cable television started. No one believed anyone would pay for television when you could watch news and entertainment for free using a signal that came through the antennas found on the roof of every home.

What I am getting at is that virtually all belief systems change over time. Even the belief system that walking in front of a car would seriously injure you could change. They are now designing concept cars made of soft material that will collapse and protect a human being should a car ever run into one.

Because no belief system is immune from evolution, you must carefully examine each and every belief that does not serve your best interest.

One should look at any ingrained belief system with a grain of skepticism. For one thing, belief systems are scientifically being challenged daily. For another, we live in a society where advertising is being deliberately designed to ingrain us with the belief that certain products will solve our problems and thus turn us into obedient and willing consumers.

Here is a big belief system that most folks carry that is not based on reality. The belief that more money, toys, possessions, vacations makes one a happy and joyous person.

The belief that accumulating more toys and possessions will make one feel happier and more satisfied is a complete fallacy. That belief system is even perpetuated by many New Age practitioners and philosophers who sell their ideas by implying that you'll be able to manifest a bunch of expensive goodies once you learn their beliefs.

In reality, more stuff will never bring you more joy. It might bring a temporary rush of happiness. But, in the long run, more possessions are just more things to take care of and be responsible for. This is proven every day when the celebrity news tells us about someone who is miserable even though he or she has a load of toys and millions in the bank.

Even when we have evidence entirely to the contrary we can and do buy into certain belief systems. A good example is the belief system that to be safe, happy, successful and content one must work hard and struggle for most of one's life. You can see proof all around you that this is not true at all. There are people all over, famous and not famous, who have never had to work hard at all and yet are very joyous, successful, content and in some cases even wealthy.

We also buy into the belief system that you need a certain level of education to be successful in a career. Yet there are plenty of examples of people who have hardly any education yet are very successful in their careers.

Many people even buy into the belief system that a certain day of the week is unpleasant because it is called Monday. How many times have you asked someone how he was feeling and replied, "Well, it's Monday" like that has anything to do with anything?

This is why you have to examine the belief systems you carry within you. You have to really look carefully at them rather than just accept them.

Here are the big three internal questions you should start asking yourself about your own belief systems.

1. Who told me this?

2. Does this belief system work in my best interest?

3. If not, why did I buy into it?

The reason this is so important is because your belief systems form the world around you. Great sages and philosophers have known and said this for years.

As James Allen put it in his landmark 1902 book, *As a Man Thinketh*:

Mind is the Master power that moulds and makes,

And Man is Mind, and evermore he takes

The tool of Thought, and, shaping what he wills,

Brings forth a thousand joys, a thousand ills:—

He thinks in secret, and it comes to pass:

Environment is but his looking-glass.

Notice that poem is actually another way of expressing of the Law of Perception.

Everything we think, feel, and experience in life is based on one belief system or another.

The body is totally obedient and will follow your belief systems like a dog on a leash. If you have a belief system that eating certain foods is bad for you and you continue to eat them you'll definitely have bad things show up in your body.

If you believe that germs are going to overpower your immune system every time someone coughs on you then most likely they will. I gave up that belief system a long time ago and I have not experienced a cold or flu in years.

It's not that I don't believe in germs. But I certainly don't believe that a couple of germs are going to be able to overpower my immune system. It doesn't make sense to me.

Plato noted back in 400BC that one of the best ways to keep your mind and body joyous and healthy is to believe it is exactly that way. "We do not cure the body with the body, we cure the body with the mind: and if the mind is confused and upset, it cannot cure anything properly."

Furthermore, those of you who have been through any major experiences with the medical profession are well aware that the diagnosis seems to change with each new person who is brought in to evaluate you.

One medical practitioner's belief system will be the replaced with another and then yet another.

So who are you to believe? The doctor that tells you, "It's probably just gas," or the one who tells you who tells you, "Perhaps it is cancer"

Before you believe either one be sure to ask the three questions.

1. Who told me this?

2. Does this belief system work in my best interest?

3. If not, why did I buy into it?

Which of those two options, gas or cancer, do you feel is in your best interest?

As I said before: your body is very obedient.

It's going to listen and obey whatever belief system you buy into.

So if I were you I would choose very carefully.

CHAPTER 8

HOW WE BLOCK JOY OUT

The trick is not how much pain you feel--but how much joy you feel. Any idiot can feel pain. Life is full of excuses to feel pain, excuses not to live, excuses, excuses, excuses.

~ Erica Jong

IT seems impossible that we could block out something as important as our real true joyous nature, doesn't it?

I mean if joy is always available all around us how could we possibly not perceive it all the time?

If something was that large is there any way we could not see it or be aware of it?

The truth is absolutely yes and I'm going to prove it to you right now.

Have you ever lived in the city or had a job near something that's very noisy like an all-night factory or the freeway? When you moved to that location you may have had a little trouble sleeping the first few nights.

But after a while an amazing thing happens. You don't even notice the noise anymore. Sure, once in a while you'll become aware of it, but mostly you will entirely be unaware of the noise. People will ask, "How can you live here?" and you will answer, "I don't really notice it anymore."

What happens is our mind turns on its filtration system and after awhile decides the excess noise is extraneous information to the task at hand so it filters out. Our mind makes a judgment and determines the very loud and intrusive sound is not necessary in your awareness.

Ponder this... if you're beautiful mind has the ability to filter out something as loud as a constant high decibel noise do you think maybe there are other things it might be filtering out as well?

Yes, there is. Something quite huge: the ever-present joy of our world.

There is a world all around us that's shouting with joy. Universal joy is flowing everywhere. It manifests as love and beauty in every direction you look. It is as beautiful as the sound of a million angels singing.

This world of joy creates new babies from love. This world of joy inspires first love. This world of joy designs beautiful sunsets and spectacular sunrises. This world of joy fills the air everywhere with its sweet aroma. This world vibrates in the flowers we walk by.

We are surrounded by manifestations of this world all the time. Most of us choose to ignore it in the same way we have conditioned ourselves to ignore the train that rumbles by every day. Yet it is there for you to look at every single day.

At one point in your life you saw this world clearly all day long. But you were very young and it's so hard to remember.

But, in spite of that, there were many times after childhood that the world of joy became so clear there was no way you could not have noticed.

When you first saw your newly born child it brought tears of joy to your eyes.

When you looked at your true love for the very first time all you could experience was the world of joy.

When you sat in stillness one day at the beach, or in the mountains, or in the desert and you watched that once in a lifetime sunset you visited that world of joy once again.

That proves it exists for you and for everyone. The question is, how much time will you devote to living there?

I have made the decision to devote the vast majority—if not all—of my day to living in the world of joy.

Have you? If not, why?

The world of joy does not come and go. It embraces us at all times.

But most of you have figured out how to filter joy completely out of your life.

It's not really all that hard to filter it out. All you have to do is listen to those voices that tell you all sorts of things you shouldn't have done, all sorts of things you're doing wrong now, and all sorts of things you're going to do wrong in the future.

Those jabbering voices in and out of your head will kill the world of joy.

Most of the time they will replace it with the world of fear.

Follow my joy techniques and you're going to learn easy techniques to quiet those voices down.

Afterwards you will discover how to see and hear the delight all around you and wonder how you ever missed it.

Chapter 9

Why The Media Cultivates An Unjoyous Perspective Of Life

"All media exist to invest our lives with artificial perceptions and arbitrary values"

~ Marshall McLuhan

WE'RE told from the time we are very young that what is happening in life is due to external influences. If we got a cold, it was because we were out in the cold breeze or caught a germ from someone.

Then, as we go to school, we are shown more and more scientific proof of why the things that happen in life are based on external influences.

So a basic foundation of our thinking is based on a common belief that we are victims on this planet. We are told that life is based on hundreds of thousands of circumstances and influences that are 100% out of our control.

If this is true, what else can you possibly be but a helpless victim?

Much of this Mass Consciousness thinking process is based on "the fact" that we are victims of circumstances. This puts most of us in the state of being permanently on the defensive.

If you look carefully at how you approach your day-to-day life, you will find that you have bought into the belief that you cannot control your own life.

This belief is reinforced into our brains every day from most every direction we look.

The news on television shows us countless victims every evening and the terrible circumstances they find themselves in. The media does all sorts of things to make sure that we are feeling completely sorry for these poor victims. This keeps us in a state of fear, as we certainly don't want to end up in their predicament.

The news also shows us an endless parade of murderers, kidnappers, and all sorts of heinous criminals. It then goes into grisly details describing exactly how the horrible things happened. Chances are the announcer will subtly suggest this horrible thing could easily happen to you if you don't watch out.

They never bother to mention that in a country of 300 million people the odds of any of these things happening to you are statistically very low. You are more likely to get hit by lightning than be personally affected by the most heinous of these crimes.

That is the truth. But that is not what molds minds and sells products.

If you make a regular diet of mass media, you can maintain your equilibrium and balance only if you remain aware of the fact that all this media programming and news comes at a price. While some programming can be educational in nature, one means or another must pay for all programming, which means ads are sold to pay for all this information and misinformation.

And the more violent the outcome the more specialized the ads. Have you ever noticed that when a program is about some horrible event there are plenty of ads for pest companies, security firms, and insurance companies?

The news is a blatant example of using folk's insecurity to sell products.

A well-known advertising specialist, Denny Hatch, recently performed a five day survey of commercials on *CBS Nightly News* (January 2, 3, 5, 8 and 9, 2008).

During his study he discovered that a total of 74 commercial messages were shown. Of those, 64 commercials, or 86%, were illness, drug, and health-related.

To quote Denny:

> What the viewer gets is a dose of news followed by doses of advertisements for drugs and other products that deal with our most intimate bodily organs, functions, fluids and excretions—all designed to play on our innermost fears.
>
> Integrated into many of the commercials are grisly side effects recounted by unctuous voice-over announcers who make sure we do not miss the possibilities of:
>
> Bowel Movements—Gas—Vomiting—Limp Penises—Leg Cramps—Headaches—Nausea—Decrease in Vision—Backaches—Four-hour Erections—Dizziness—Runny Nose—Decrease in Semen—Unexplained Muscle Pain—Sudden Loss of Blood Pressure—Gambling Urges—Fainting—Liver Problems—Chest Pain—Trouble Urinating—Drowsiness—Sexual Urges—Diarrhea—Prostate Cancer—Cataract Surgery—Falling asleep while driving—Upset Stomach— The need to see a doctor right away!
>
> You are socked with one of these grisly litanies four to six times in the course of the half-hour broadcast.

Do you think maybe listening to all these horrible possibilities on a nightly basis will make one feel joyous… or the opposite?

It is not the media's job to discriminate between the fact and fiction or represent life the way life truly is.

No, the media's job is to grab our attention and sell us things.

After all, the sellers of products, politics and ideologies pay the bills.

Like most of us who've worked a job, the media simply does what the "boss" tells them to do. The media's "bosses" are the sponsors of the shows. When we have a job we like to make the boss happy. The way to make the sponsors happy is to sell lots of products. It really is quite simple when you think about it.

Whether it is a drama, comedy, a talk show, a reality show, the news, the award shows, they all have the same purpose. Their purpose is to keep your attention long enough, strongly enough, to make you desire things that you do not have so you will purchase them.

The media certainly isn't evil in any way for doing this. They are simply doing what pays the bills.

It's our choice whether we want to watch it and accept it or not. It certainly isn't required. Whether you decide to watch television or not, you can bring more joy into your life by simply being aware of this fact. The job of media is to make you receptive to whatever the sponsor is selling.

I can hear you asking, "How does showing horrible crimes make people want to buy things?" That is an excellent question.

On the surface it certainly doesn't seem like those sorts of stories are going to help sell another six-pack of beer.

But that is exactly the effect those stories have, especially over the long run. Repeated exposure to all of these horrible and dreadful things makes people feel unsafe, insecure and discontent.

That is the perfect state of mind to get a prospective buyer into. When someone feels discontent he or she is very easy to sell things to. They want something that will take those feelings away so they will purchase things (or even ideas) they've been conditioned to believe will cure their discomfort.

The truth of the matter is that the more safe, secure, joyous and content you feel the less interested you are in changing things around you by buying things or following "leaders."

Those who sell their agenda to you are well aware that satisfied, happy and contented people are virtually impossible to influence.

And, like the Rolling Stones song says, those who are interested in selling you constant streams of new products are certainly not interested in your "satisfaction".

Those that sell us the products are very talented. They "program" us to believe we need something new and exciting every day. Only a few mega corporations own the different forms of major media (TV, newspapers, radio, movies, billboards). This allows the different forms of media to all work together to "program" the viewers and listeners.

The advertising firms used by these major corporations are masters at coordinating the various different types of media to deliver a consistent message that will produce feelings of fear, discontent and longing.

These companies spend millions of dollars a year researching exactly how our mind and feelings work, and how we can be manipulated to buy their products.

Imagine how much research goes in to making sure an ad is effective when a 30-second television commercial can cost over $1 million per showing. That research includes doing psychological and physiological profiles of what goes on inside a person while they watch those ads. What emotions are being stimulated? What feelings is the person going through?

These folks can afford the absolute best psychologists and analysis money can buy. They use them to sell products to you. It is a smart business decision.

If that means they are using the media to make your life feel insecure, upset, fearful, paranoid, angry, jealous, then so be it.

They are simply doing their job.

But that doesn't mean you have to pay attention.

Personally I gave up television years ago, hardly read newspapers and only listen to radio that I get through my satellite that has no commercials and very little commentary.

I'm not interested in their "programming," thank you. That's just my personal choice. For me, it works.

However, if you enjoy television—and many good people do—ask yourself how it feels to watch certain programs. Do you feel good afterward? Would you feel better if you clicked the mute button every time the ads came on?

Could you switch to another channel the moment you notice a tightening in your chest? What if you watched "Nature" instead of "CSI"? Would beautiful animals and scenery make you feel better than graphic depictions of murder and rotting body parts?

The point is to get a handle on how being an observer affects your life.

I realized that for myself making a regular diet of television was exhausting and disheartening, so I stopped watching. You may choose another way to limit the influence of the corporation fed mass media.

The choice is yours but one thing is key: be an active rather than passive observer.

Chapter 10

Big Things To Be Grateful For

In the hopes of reaching the moon men fail to see the flowers that blossom at their feet.

~ Albert Schweitzer

MANY of us embrace a warped perspective of life along the lines the lyrics of that old song that goes "you and me it against the world, sometimes it's just like you and me against the world."

As soon as we enter school they teach us how existing on this planet is simply a matter of survival. Pretty depressing outlook when you think about it.

Thank goodness this belief system—like so much of the stuff we learn when we are young—is a myth.

In truth, if the world were actually "against you" you wouldn't have survived a microsecond on this planet.

As a matter of fact, you wouldn't have been conceived in the first place.

The truth is the world embraced you. You were conceived out of love and passion.

And from the moment of your conception thousands of people started working for your benefit.

The doctors, nurses and all the other health care professionals immediately got involved to make sure your birth was smooth and safe. Dozens of people started sewing material together that would later become your baby clothes. Workers all over the country started building your crib, your toys, your baby bottle, and hundreds of other items you would need as a baby.

Not to mention those that built the house your parents were living in, the car they drove and all of the thousands of things that contributed to their lives while they were bringing you into this wonderful world.

But it doesn't stop there.

Let's not forget the thousands of farmers who worked so hard every day growing crops, the migrant farm workers who harvested those crops, the truckers that took the food to the factories and all of the workers who processed and bottled your baby food.

Or those that created and maintained the various water, electrical, heat, medicine, education and thousands of other benefits necessary for your growth.

Yes, not only did the world fully embrace you, but also untold thousands of people you never met worked and created things directly for your benefit.

This is the truth about life.

Every day thousands of people are contributing to you in one way or another. Once you start realizing this it becomes one heck of a lot easier to attain a state of joy.

Let me give you an example of how this perspective can be put into use every day.

When the average person goes to the store and buys themselves a can of tuna the mental processes are pretty simple. Chances are she experiences the situation as, "I just spent my hard-earned money buying myself a can of tuna. It sure is expensive. I can't believe they charge so much for it."

When I go and buy a can of tuna I see things much differently. I see hundreds of hardworking people making that product available to me. My vision starts with an ocean teeming with life. I see dozens of fishermen out on a boat freezing in the pouring rain throwing nets out to grab a few of those fish. Those women and men bring the nets in and the tuna goes down below in the boat where it is prepared by dozens of other workers. Then the tuna is transported by truckers over thousands of miles of road. There another set of folks in the grocery business unpack the boxes and put the tuna out on the shelf.

All of these people worked incredibly hard just so I could enjoy a tuna sandwich.

Is this an amazingly beautiful world or what?

More importantly, how could I even survive a week in the world without all of the millions of other folks working everyday for my benefit?

The same applies to almost anything one consumes, uses, buys, drives, lives in, works at, and the list goes on and on.

Think about the experience of going to a movie. I always enjoy the experience even if I don't like the movie all that much. Why?

Because to me it is completely wonderful that thousands of people worked a couple of years and spent a couple of hundred million dollars or so creating this movie just so I could be entertained for a few hours.

Isn't that worthy of being joyful?

I know this perspective may sound a little bit over-the-top to you. But again... what works in your best interest?

There certainly is no need to look at things this way. But there is also no need to look at things in a negative light.

Like everything this is absolutely your choice. If you feel it's is your best interest to look at the world as this place where everybody and everything is against you then it is certainly your right to think and feel that way.

On the other hand, if you feel it is in your best interest to look at the world as a place that is embracing you it is just as much your right to see it that way instead.

If you remain aware that multitudes of people are contributing to your benefit every day; if you simply remember that every single small thing that comes into your life has an incredible back story which involves the thousands of people necessary for its creation, you will be not only more joyous, but closer to recognizing the truth of your existence here.

So I ask you, which way of looking at things do you feel is in your best interest?

Chapter 11

Step 1: Stop Throwing Your Joy Away

If you are disturbed by any external thing, it is not this that disturbs you, but your own judgment about it.

~ Marcus Aurelius

THIS is by far the biggest obstacle to joy in your life.

If you ask the average person why it is they are not joyful more of the time, they will give you a litany of reasons. These reasons will usually have to do with things that are happening in the outside world: health, career, politics, the price of gas, and problems with relatives or relationships. The list literally can go on and on forever.

As a stated earlier, if being in joy were dependent on the circumstances of the outside world it would be an almost impossible goal.

The world simply is. It will do what it is going to do on a daily basis. Many of the things that occur in this world you are probably not going to agree with.

You can accept that fact and be joyous. Or you can fight that fact and be upset.

Either way the "fact" will not change.

If you believe that the circumstances and people you don't agree with have the power to keep you from joy, I have news for you: that belief is a total fantasy.

I hate to sound blunt. But it is the truth.

Joy is a state of mind. It is not the end result of a bunch of circumstances all working out exactly the way you want.

It is dependent on you, not the outside world. No one else and nothing else in this world has the ability to create your state of mind but you.

If that is the case, then why aren't you enjoying life all of the time? What is the obstacle that keeps you from a state of constant joy?

Well, folks, I am going to admit that what you are facing is a huge obstacle. It's an obstacle I faced for 45 years. I asked myself over and over again why I was not in joy. I looked high and low for the obstacle that was keeping me from the joy within.

When I found it I was flabbergasted. The obstacle was so close it was actually very hard to find. It was staring me right in the face.

There is a famous line that first appeared in a cartoon during World War II. That line is, "We have met the enemy and he is us."

In a nutshell, here is the biggest obstacle to embracing your joy: Your willingness to throw it away!

That's right: *your* willingness to throw it away.

The reason you don't have it around all of the time actually comes down to the fact that you don't value it enough to keep it around.

It's certainly isn't that you don't know what joy feels like. You've been there thousands of times in your life.

When it was right in front of you why didn't you hang onto it? Have you ever thought about that?

Was it because something in the outside world changed and took your joy away? Did another person come and steal it from you, perhaps?

No. None of those things happened.

What did happen is this... you decided there was another way you were going to feel besides joy.

You replaced that wonderful feeling of joy with anger, judgment, resentment, fear, worry or any of a dozen other emotions that can crowd joy completely out of the picture.

I know it sounds strange but in truth when you left your joy it was because the new distasteful emotion became more appealing to you than joy.

You were seduced into the excitement of the dark side.

Excitement. That is a big key to this mystery.

Excitement is the "reward" that the emotions of anger, judgment, resentment, fear, worry, hate all have to offer you.

In the second *Star Wars* movie, Yoda says to Luke, "Excitement, a Jedi seeks this not."

When I was young and saw that movie I had no clue what he meant. As I grew older and wiser I began to realize exactly what he meant.

As a society we tend to like to be excited. And in many areas of life excitement is a wonderful, vibrant and enlightening experience.

But when it comes to feelings and emotions, excitement tends to obscure your joy.

A state of joy tends to be more of a state of peace then excitement.

Because of our constant thirst for excitement and stimulation we tend to throw a state of joy away in favor of something that gives us more juice.

Let me give you a concrete example.

You're having a wonderful day and you decide to go over to the mall to get a bit of shopping done. You are going to get a nice gift for your sweetheart. It makes you feel wonderful to think of the reaction when your sweetheart sees this. You have a big smile on your face as you pull into the parking lot and see a space very near the entrance. As you start to pull into the parking space a car cuts you off from the other direction and zooms into the parking space.

You have just hit what I call, "The moment of decision."

You have a definite choice standing right in front of you.

There's a lyric in a song by the rock group Devo that I remember at times like these: "Don't be fooled by what you see, you've got two ways to go."

There are two paths you can take at this point. You can continue smiling and drive down another row and find another parking space. I mean, after all, what difference does it make if you have to walk a little farther? In fact, it might do you some good.

That is the peaceful and joyous path. Forgive and forget the minor irritations that happen in life and move onward.

Or you can take the exciting path. You can get all upset and angry.

"How dare that person cut me off! How could he do such a thing to me? What a jerk! Boy, I feel like punching his...!"

That's all very exciting. It really gets your juices going. It's even, in kind of a perverted way, fun. But joyous it certainly is not.

You have just taken your precious gift of joy and thrown out the window. In its place you have filled your mind with anger and resentment.

More importantly...you have given the person who pulled into the parking space ahead of you total power over your life.

You had handed the keys to your state of mind and frame of reference to another individual.

You have put yourself into the equation as a victim of another person.

So, in my opinion, you have given your strength to that person.

But it is exciting, isn't it? Feeling that adrenaline rise. Getting that rush of self-righteousness. Feeling justified in your anger. All of these things are exciting.

The excitement is so seducing it is almost irresistible.

But is it in your best interest?

That's a question only you can answer.

For me the answer is that it is definitely not in my best interest to hand the keys of my state of mind, my peace and joy, to another individual or even a random circumstance in life.

When I am in a state of joy I am in complete control. When I am in a state of fear, anger, hate, resentment, or victim hood, then someone or something else is in control.

I choose to remain in control. How about you?

Whatever you've chosen in the past is irrelevant. The beauty is, you can choose again. Starting right now, if you want.

CHAPTER 12

STEP 2: IDENTIFY THE TWO VOICES IN YOUR MIND

Heed the still small voice that so seldom leads us wrong, and never into folly.

~ Marquise du Deffand

AS I mentioned earlier, we all have two voices in our mind. Great writers throughout the centuries have written stories about the conflict between these two voices. Some belief systems call these voices the higher self and the ego.

I'm going to simplify things quite a bit from the complexities of trying to sort out which voice comes from the higher self and which voice comes from the ego.

I'm going to do that by using the same analogy for those voices that one of the great writers used in a story you are most likely familiar with.

Peter Pan.

I know, it sounds kind of silly. Peter Pan is just a fairy tale for kids, right?

No, not at all. Actually, J.M. Barrie wrote the play *Peter Pan* as a tale entirely for adults back in the late 1800s. In those days children didn't even go to plays. Therefore, it was not written as a children's book or as a children's cartoon as Disney would like people to believe.

Because it was a play, paying adults had to want to come and see it in order for it to have survived! If it had been written for children, we never would have heard about it because it would've been a flop.

So what possible message could a play like Peter Pan have for adults?

Like everything else, it really depends upon how you look at it. Personally, I think Peter Pan is one of the greatest pieces of literature ever written. I hold it right up there with the *Bible, Don Quixote,* and another alleged children's book *Alice in Wonderland.*

To refresh your memory or in case you are unfamiliar with the story, here are the basics.

Peter Pan is introduced at the beginning of the play like this. "All children grow up, except one."

The play opens when Peter Pan meets Wendy and her younger siblings, as they are about to go to bed. He says he wants to take them to a brand-new world called Neverland. When they ask how they'll get there, he says, "We'll fly, of course."

But the children have the same problem most adults on this planet seem to have. They simply cannot believe a human being can go beyond their self-imposed limitations and fly.

Yet when they see Peter fly they are astonished. And naturally when they see someone else do it they want to do it as well. Even more to the point, once they see someone else accomplish it they know it is something that can be done.

So they asked Peter. "How can we fly?"

And Peter Pan says with an impish smile, "It's easy. You just think happy thoughts."

And the children fill their heads with happy thoughts. And guess what? They start flying!

When people come to me and say, "Ed, I'm totally in the dumps. I feel like I'm sinking into a world of hurt and pain. Is there anyway I can raise myself above this?"

Just like Peter I want to say to them, "It's easy. You just think happy thoughts"

I don't, of course, because I know it would sound insensitive at best. However, the fact is, if you can allow yourself to "think happy thoughts" you would find yourself a whole lot lighter.

If you can allow yourself to spend more time thinking "happy thoughts" not only would you be in a constant state of joy, but you would be happier, healthier and more productive. Now that's my idea of "flying" through life!

We'll talk a lot about thinking happy thoughts in this book, but now let's get back to Peter Pan.

Because Peter never lost touch with the joy, wonder and innocence of his inner child he never grew old and could literally soar through life.

Peter Pan represents one of the voices that exist in all of us. The voice that is sometimes called the higher self.

Yet Peter had a nemesis. A name most of us know. This nemesis was Captain Hook.

Captain Hook represents everything that Peter Pan isn't. Captain Hook represents the other voice that exists in all of us. The one called the ego.

Captain Hook is constantly in fear. Why? Because Captain Hook has a crocodile after him 24 hours a day. He would always know when that crocodile was near and ready to take his life because the crocodile had a ticking clock inside of him. Whenever the crocodile would get close, Hook could hear that clock ticking away and the fear would become so overwhelming that Hook couldn't think straight.

That crocodile had already taken Captain Hook's hand. That is why he had a hook in its place. The memory of losing his hand, now replaced with a hook, haunted the poor Captain constantly.

Captain Hook represents a change that manifests in all of us as we grow. It was no accident that Barrie chose a hook as a replacement for the character's hand.

Symbolism tells us that the hand represents opening. An open hand is like an open heart. It is ready to accept and it is ready to let go. It doesn't hang onto things forever. It examines and enjoys things and then lets them go.

On the other hand (bad pun), a hook grabs everything in sight. A hook permanently holds onto anything that its snags. A hook cannot let go even if it wants to

Interestingly, the only way a hook can release anything is with the assistance of a hand.

As we lose our childhood innocence we become less like Peter Pan and more and more like Captain Hook. We grab onto everything and we don't let go. We accumulate feelings, emotions, material possessions, resentments, anger, and judgments.

And the more we hook onto these things, the more we fear the crocodile with the ticking clock inside of it. That clock is our allocated time on earth. The more stuff we hang onto the more fear we will have of that clock.

We already resent the "crocodile" because we think it took our hand (our inner child). We also know that "crocodile" is eventually going to get each and every one of us. We all know for absolute certain that we only have so many ticks of the clock.

There is only one way to beat the fear of the crocodile. You must change from the perspective of Captain Hook to the perspective of Peter Pan by reclaiming your joy and innocence.

Peter Pan had no fear of the crocodile or the ticking of the life clock.

This is dramatically shown in the play. Captain Hook gains a total advantage over Peter Pan and holds a sword right to his throat. Captain Hook says with a sneer, "You are now going to die, Peter Pan!"

And Peter looks right into Captain Hook's eyes with an irreverent smile and says, "Dying will be such a grand adventure." Peter refused to let fear stop his enjoyment of the moment, even with a sword to his throat.

Talk about having the right perspective on things.

There is an important lesson in this for all of us.

Inside of us there lives a beautiful, innocent, loving, trusting, wide-eyed child who sees everything that happens in life as a grand adventure. Let's call that child Peter Pan.

Whether you are aware of it or not, that child is pushing hard to come to the surface. That child doesn't hang on to hurt. That child does not hang on to anger or resentment. That child is fully aware that this world we live in is a beautiful, magical place full of incredible adventures, joy, wonderful people and laughter.

That child wants to share with everyone. That child wants to laugh and play and have fun.

Inside each one of us there are is also a bitter and resentful Captain Hook. He lives in constant fear of the ticking of the clock. He grabs onto everything in sight with his hook.

He bitterly dreams of better times in better places. He judges everyone and everything he sees as, "out to get him." He knows that this world is full of dark and ugly people. He refuses to let go of anger, hurt, fear or resentment, and he will always take advantage of others and never share.

Just like the Captain Hook of the fairy tale, your internal Captain Hook has only one goal in life. One overwhelming goal that occupies all of his thoughts...

That goal is to kill Peter Pan once and for all.

Will you let him?

Will you let your internal Captain Hook's bitter, angry, resentful voice drown out and kill the loving, positive, joyous voice of your internal Peter Pan?

It is your choice: you can focus your attention on your inner Peter Pan voice or pay attention to your inner Captain Hook.

Start paying close attention to those voices inside of you and what they are saying. Instead of thinking of it as *THE* voice in your head, think of it is the two voices in your head. Believe me there are two, no question.

It should not take you very long to recognize them. Once you do it's your decision on which one you want to focus on.

Don't worry if you've been hearing Captain Hook in your mind lately a lot more than you've been hearing Peter Pan. Your internal Peter Pan can never die. He's a much bigger part of you than you realize.

He does go into hiding sometimes. He hid from me for years.

By taking the steps I outline in *Unstoppable Joy*, you will soon know exactly how to find him.

Here's the first hint: he will only come out if you want him to.

CHAPTER 13

STEP 3: CONTROL YOUR CRITICAL 60 SECONDS

Everyday is a renewal, every morning the Joy you feel is life.

--Gertrude Stein

IN my opinion, one of the most important steps to assuring a joyful day starts the moment you become conscious in the morning. Those seconds when your brain first becomes aware after sleep are what I call, "The Critical 60."

This is, by far, the easiest time to set a reference point for your day. If you can get past those first critical 60 seconds, and maintain joy through them, you will have an upper hand on the circumstances that may challenge you during the rest of your day.

This is because something amazing happens every night when you go to sleep. Your brain goes into a housekeeping mode. It reviews all of the thoughts, feelings and emotions you've had during your previous day and determines which are worth keeping and which should be tossed.

Remember what we discussed in Chapter 6: At any one moment in time you are surrounded by approximately four million sensory inputs that you can choose to focus on. Because with all of the millions of sensory inputs we receive on a daily basis our brain would absolutely overload if it retained every single one of them, so our mind has to go through a sifting process to eliminate the extraneous information and feelings as we sleep.

The expression "I will sleep on it" is based on our intuitive knowledge of how the brain does its daily cleanup routine. We know that when we sleep the extraneous information is removed and the decision is made easier.

Okay, now let's get back to "The Critical 60."

This wonderful process our brain goes through every night gives us a tremendous opportunity. Our brain just removed the information it considers useless. Besides stuff like what traffic was like or who was on the cover of the *National Enquirer*, a lot of information the brain gets rid of is literally mental garbage; i.e. bad feelings, resentments, useless judgments, and all sorts of things we might've put in our brain that do not serve our best interest in the coming day.

So, in a way, our brain has prepared us for a state of joy by eliminating much of the information that takes delight away from us.

We literally wake up refreshed and renewed.

The problem is most of us start thinking about exactly the wrong things the moment we awake and so revert back to where we were the day before.

I know I certainly used to do that. I can remember when my first thoughts in the morning would be of all of the problems and difficulties I had to face that day. I would imagine all of the personality conflicts I was going to have to deal with or start to worry about the bills I had to pay.

In other words, I would take this beautiful blank slate and immediately start filling it back up with garbage.

And then I learned through much research, and tons of personal experience, that the first minute of consciousness sets the stage for your entire day.

Yes, it's hard not to think of those challenging things. With me it felt completely natural. It was like a knee-jerk reaction. I'd wake up, I'd start thinking about problems and difficulties.

Folks, there is a much better way.

Would you like to know a simple method to make every morning seem beautiful? What if I told you there was a fail safe technique that will lay out the day ahead in a soft welcoming manner; a way that will make your path so much smoother and bring so much sunshine into your life.

So what the heck way am I talking about? Does it involve prayer? Does it involve meditation? Actually, no. It doesn't involve anything religious or spiritual in the slightest degree.

It's also quite simple to do, but it can be amazingly difficult to remember to do it, particularly in those first few seconds of consciousness.

Are you ready for a secret to a more joyous life? Try this...

The second you awake, as soon as you become conscious, realize you have been given an incredible gift.

That incredible gift is *another day of life on this planet*. There was no guarantee it was going to be here last night when you went to sleep. And here it is: another day to enjoy.

Yep, the crocodile didn't get you last night. The ticking of the clock goes on.

I think that's a pretty amazing thing myself because one day it will not be the truth. The ticking will stop, the crocodile will smile a satisfied grin, and it will all be over.

No more enjoying this body. No more embracing your children. No more being around your friends and relatives in physical form. No more sunny days, no more starry nights.

Do you think the fact you didn't lose all that between last night and this morning is worth being grateful for?

It certainly was not guaranteed. It is a gift. Every single day is a new gift.

I know this is harder than it seems sometimes. Our minds tend to be a little bit jumbled and confused first thing in the morning. If you're like most people, you trained yourself for decades to start worrying first thing in the morning so it's going to take some fortitude to change to this sort of mindset at the very start of the day.

Yet I can guarantee you it will be worth a thousand times more than the effort.

In virtually every self-help method and spiritual book you'll find references to the life-changing power of having an, "Attitude of Gratitude." Holding gratitude in your heart has been proven for thousands of years to create joy and peace in one's life.

Okay, I know, you have bills to pay, your marriage is kaput, your job is on the line – yes there are challenges in this life.

But blessings are also abundant. All you have to do is have the discipline to make a habit of noticing them *first*. Believe me, once you attain this habit the rest of the stuff will either cease to matter or turn around.

Personally, I think you owe it to yourself to take the first 60 seconds of your day to be grateful. I don't care whether you believe in God or not, to not be grateful for the gift of life every single day is like shooting yourself in the foot.

Everyone will have to choose what method works best for him or her, but here is how I start my day. I open my eyes, take a deep breath and say, "Thank you, thank you, I am still alive. I get to see another beautiful day. I get to hear the wonderful voices of my friends. I get to smell the flowers. I get to see the sky. I get to pet my beautiful kitty once again. Thank you, thank you, thank you."

But it doesn't stop there. That's just the beginning.

Because after that I start flooding my mind with other things I have to be thankful for: my health, a warm roof over my head, a comfortable bed, food in the refrigerator to make breakfast from, supportive friends and even all the marvelous people who read my writing.

It's a very simple process. One at a time, I bring up an image of something I'm thankful for and I simply say, "thank you." It doesn't matter who I am saying "Thank you" to, what matters is being grateful.

By the time my "Critical 60" is done, I have brought dozens and dozens of wonderful images to my mind and have expressed gratitude for each and every one of them.

This simple 60-second exercise can make a staggeringly dramatic change in everything that happens afterward.

Why?

Because we tend to look at the circumstances of our day based on the viewpoint we developed as we awoke. If we start with worry, it has a domino effect and soon more things to worry about are created. If we start with an "Attitude of Gratitude," it will also create a domino style chain reaction, thus bringing more good into our day.

It's your choice. The beauty of it is you can choose to start every day with the "Critical 60" exercise and change your life in the process.

CHAPTER 14

STEP 4: CAREFULLY CHOOSE YOUR MEMORIES

Better by far you should forget and smile, Than you should remember and be sad.

--Christina Rossetti

WHERE do happy thoughts and horrible thoughts come from? Do they just "pop" into our heads?

I know it seems that way sometimes but in truth here is where they come from.

We choose them from thousands of available thoughts.

Your mind is a giant depository up images, sounds, thoughts, memories, and feelings.

Imagine your mind like a giant Library of Congress, with dozens of incredible hallways extending in every direction. Each of these hallways is full of bookshelves.

Each of these bookshelves contains thousands of videotapes. And on each one of these videotapes is a memory of an incident in your life or an event that you've repeatedly thought about that may happen in the future.

So here is your mind like a giant, beautiful library teeming with hundreds of thousands of videotapes, each one a replay of a small section of your life.

You are already aware of this. Nearly every day you will go into that library and pull out something and replay it. We all do this. Some of us do it virtually all the time.

Unfortunately, lots of us seem to have a habit of playing tapes that are not exactly pleasant to watch. I don't exactly know why we like to do this, but we do.

When you are in a state of misery I can almost bet you are picking up one of those tapes and you are playing it over and over in your mind. And if you're in misery I can guarantee the tape you are playing is of either something bad that happened in the past, or something bad that you fear may happen in the future.

Have you ever done that? Have you ever sat and repeated the same tape over and over again, re living and projecting those horrible experiences (or imagined experience in the future) and continuously watching again and again?

I know I certainly used to do that. I suspect maybe you do too.

Here is the solution. The same huge library of tapes that was used to reinforce your misery can be used to rebuild your joy. You just have to change the shelf you are looking at.

Because I know a lot about the library in my mind, I can make an educated guess about the library that's in yours.

There are thousands of tapes to choose from in this library. So, when you find yourself in a depressed or miserable state of mind, do yourself a favor. For just a few minutes put down the particular tape you're watching and see what else you can find in this library.

Maybe I can be of some assistance...

Ah-Ha... I believe I see an interesting tape over here! Why look at this. This is the tape of the time when you looked in the eyes of your newborn child. Wow, what a joyous feeling that tape brings! You can play that one over and over again if you like.

Hey, here is another one! That was the day you fell in love with your sweetheart. Boy, that sure was an incredible day, wasn't it? Remember how joyful it felt?

Check out this tape over here! I think that's a tape of your daughter's graduation. You were so proud and happy. Remember your delight when the dean called out her name?

There's a tape of the day your friends gave you that wonderful surprise party, and another of that beautiful week you spent on vacation in Paradise.

Holy mackerel! There are countless tapes in here of incredibly good things and joyous feelings you experienced in your life. We could spend days and days in here just enjoying these wonderful tapes and the joyous feelings they are bringing. Even if we spent weeks at this we will barely scratch the surface of potential "warm fuzzys" available in this section of the library.

Okay, so where were we?

Oh, that's right. We were busy being miserable and unhappy. So I guess we should get back to what we were doing?

To do that we will have to go find the tape we were first watching. You know, the one with all of that horrible stuff on it.

Do you really want to start watching that one again?

When we have all of these thousands of delightful, empowering and loving memories from which to choose, why would we want to continue to run the tape that makes us feel bad?

Who knows? But we sure tend to do that.

The important point is those memories don't just come... they are *chosen* by you.

Because it is you who decide which tapes to put on and watch. No one else has the power to choose a memory and put it in your mind. Only you can make the choice to be miserable or happy.

These memories and thoughts of fear of the future don't randomly come popping out of nowhere. Either we create them or we choose them from our library. In any case we are the ones in charge.

So next time you find yourself going over and over unhappy memories or unhappy feelings ask yourself if there's a better tape you can find in that library.

There is no reason you can't offset the effect of watching the horrible tape by watching something more uplifting for a while. Yes, there are unpleasant things we have to deal with, but there's no reason we should limit our viewing to a single negative subject. And since you run the machine, you can watch the tape of joyous feelings, wonder and beautiful memories over and over again just like you watch the other one.

Heck, you can watch the tapes of pleasant memories all the time if you want to. I certainly try to.

It's all a matter of choice. And the beauty of it is... You can always choose again.

CHAPTER 15

STEP 5: STOP PLACING EMOTIONAL BETS AND COMPARING EVERYTHING

There are two times in a man's life when he should not speculate: when he can't afford it and when he can.

--Mark Twain

I have never really thought of myself as a gambling man. I used to go to Reno, Las Vegas and similar places like many people do. But, unlike the folks I was traveling with, I would usually get bored of gambling after about 20 minutes.

It never really excited me to sit on one side of the table and hand my money over to the gal on the other side.

I would rather spend my money on entertainment.

It wasn't until my mid 40s that I realized that my perception of myself as not being a gambler was completely wrong. That is because I placed many bets every single day.

I placed emotional bets. I placed bets on the outcome of nearly every single situation in my life.

Emotional bets.

Here is what I mean. If a situation in life went the way I wanted it to I would be excited, giddy, happy and delighted. On the other hand, I would become disappointed, dejected, angry, irritable, defeatist and, in extreme cases, depressed if a situation didn't go the way I wanted.

What this did was create a situation where my life was a series of emotional highs and lows. It would be a constant state of being either up or down.

Once I realized what I was doing it became obvious the damage this emotional betting was doing to my Joy and Peace. So I decided I was going to quit placing emotional bets.

I decided to cultivate a new way of looking at life's challenges. If something went the way I wanted that was absolutely fantastic. And if I had to deal with something that wasn't going the way I wanted that was okay as well.

Of course, it's human nature to work and strive to have things go the direction one wants. But if for some reason one gets sidetracked, one certainly shouldn't let it create a negative emotional state that will affect one's productivity.

It's simply a smart way of managing your emotions. Life is going to create situations for you that you aren't going to necessarily want. You don't have a choice about that.

But you do have a choice about how you're going to react to it. Your mind is the ultimate decision-maker.

That simple change in perspective can make a monumental change in your life.

In my work with people I find this "emotional betting" is a very common state of mind in our society. I would go so far as to call it normal as far as mass consciousness is concerned.

Now here are two lies that directly tie in with emotional betting.

THE LIE OF COMPARISON

Comparison is entirely a tool of the ego and the other edge of judgment's sword. Whatever enjoyment one may be experiencing, the ego is sure to try and pull out another time when the experience was "better."

Whether it be a wonderful meal, and incredible sports event, a concert, a play, a movie or even a personal accomplishment, they can all be ruined by the utterance either verbal or mental of a simple phrase, "This is really wonderful, but not as good as..."

There you go! The moment is gone.

The entire viewpoint of your situation has now been changed to something else. Let's face it: the moment isn't as good now; the accomplishment not as great; the meal not as tasty; the concert not quite as good.

Here's the kicker. What you're comparing it to is a lie! Our minds don't remember any past situation with enough accuracy to be able to compare the taste of one meal with another meal. Remember those extraneous facts I mentioned in Chapter 6, the ones that get removed as we sleep? Well, guess what, the specifics of a meal are among them.

Sorry, folks, it just isn't possible to accurately compare. There are too many variations in each experience to make a qualitative comparison from one moment to the next. For example, did you know even city water changes in quality from one day to the next and therefore a restaurant's soup may taste different even if it is the same kind of soup? These variations also apply to the company you are with, the weather, the state of mind you happen to be in, the smells, and all the other sorts of things that vary from moment to moment, often in a single day!

The truth is, the mind cannot isolate out the one single factor in a certain experience that made it different from another, so the ego defines experiences as better or worse. This limitation in our brain's ability to be specific means the ego cannot offer any sort of unbiased opinion in "real time" and therefore comparison is moot.

There is the phrase that is the key. Real time. The moment in time we all know as now. Which leads us to another lie.

THE LIE OF THE FUTURE

I never think of the future. It comes soon enough.

~ Albert Einstein

In truth there is no other time but right now.

The future, which we love to spend so much time thinking about, is made up of nothing but speculation. Not only do we not know what's going to be going on five years from now, we don't have the ability to know what's going to happen five microseconds from now.

This wonderful game of life we are all playing is the greatest game ever conceived.

It is the ultimate game of chance. Every single factor of your reality can change at every moment of your life.

Many of us have lives that will end completely unexpectedly. Car accidents and slips in bathtubs take lives every day.

In the area where I've spent most of my life, the Pacific Northwest, we adore our trees and forests. It's one of the reasons so many people move here.

They aren't always 100% benign. Life presented me with an enlightening lesson one snowy December night about four years ago.

I was walking through the forest near my house to get my mail. I was in a state of bliss.

The silence of the night was broken by a sound as loud as thunder. An old, hundred-foot pine tree about 20 feet away from me had just had one snowflake too many land on it.

The weight of one tiny snowflake combined with the previously accumulated snow to bring the tree down in the blink of an eye. I heard a huge crack. I felt the angry fury of dozens of twigs and branches whipping my body and clothes.

Then *BOOM!* The ground itself shook and trembled as tens of thousands of pounds of the majestic tree landed just a few feet in front of me.

Yet I was still alive. The crocodile missed his opportunity once again.

What did I feel? Fear?

Nope – I felt gratitude.

I thanked the universe immediately for giving me yet more time to laugh and play on this planet. I laughed at the realization that for all of us the end of this beautiful existence can happen in an instant.

A few steps further and I would have been another interesting statistic.

But luckily, I wasn't ahead of myself that frigid night.

Had I been rushing to my mailbox a bit faster; had I been just a little more impatient; had I been driving towards some goal in "the future," I wouldn't be here to tell you this wonderful tale.

How about you? Are you feeling a few steps ahead of yourself?

Are you enjoying what's going on around you right now or are you thinking about "the future?"

I hate to be so blunt, but I don't know how else to tell you: *The future simply does not exist.*

Here's proof that starts with a question: When does the future arrive?

Now, think of any particular time in the future that you are sure is going to come. For the sake of argument, let's say the moment when your alarm goes off tomorrow morning.

Next, remember that during all the time between then and now that "one snowflake too many" might land on your life.

Only tomorrow morning, *if* and when you're able to respond when your alarm goes off, you'll be able to say to yourself, "Ed was wrong, the future is real because it is here right now."

And I will smile and totally agree with you. Because it is here... *RIGHT NOW.*

So I come back to my statement again. There is no future. There is only *Right Now!* Every single time without fail there is nothing else but now. And there never will be.

Which brings us to one of the most important points about living joyously. There is only one way to have a joyous future. And that is to learn to be joyous **right now**. And there is only one way to have a wonderful life. That is to learn to have a wonderful life **right now**. And there is only one way to have a life filled with love. That is to learn to have a life filled with love **right now**.

Think of what a marvelous secret this is to realize. You have the power to change your life at any time. You have the power to change your life once and for all. In your hands is the key to everything you desire. And that key is in your hand **right now**.

This is one of the truths behind *The Secret*. All of the manifestation techniques taught by anyone, anywhere, are simply versions of getting you to change your perceptions about life right now.

That is all it takes.

The downside is that unless one makes the change in attitude right now, none of the manifestation techniques can work at all.

Why? Because nothing in the future can happen without acceptance in the now.

That's what I call the "The Manifestation Shortcut." I have actually printed it out and put it up on my wall so I don't forget it.

"Nothing in the future can manifest without acceptance in the now"

What does that mean for your future happiness?

It means that the phrase "Future Happiness" has no meaning at all because there is no future.

I know folks who sacrificed nearly all of their present happiness in their quest for "Future Happiness." They never found it because it simply cannot exist. They might as well have sacrificed their present happiness in a quest for Leprechaun gold. Actually, I would put higher odds on finding Leprechaun gold than future happiness.

Because, as the song says, "yesterday was once tomorrow, and tomorrow is now today." And, because every moment was once the future, nothing in the future can happen without acceptance in the now.

Once you understand this universal law things become much simpler. In other words, to manifest joy, happiness, love or anything else you desire you must accept it right now.

The reason you are not experiencing joy in the moment has more to do with pushing it into some imagined future than it does with any shortage of availability in the now.

CHAPTER 16

STEP 6: FREE YOURSELF WITH FORGIVENESS

The more a man knows, the more he forgives.

--Catherine the Great

I call forgiveness the "F" word.

In fact, my personal experience indicates that talking about forgiveness seems to offend a lot of people more than the other "F" word.

This amazes me completely.

You don't forgive others for their benefit. You forgive others for your *own* benefit. In other words, you forgive others because it is in your best interest.

When I first started my spiritual journey back when I was 20 years old, I read an intriguing quote by the great Paramahansa Yogananda. I didn't really have a clue to understanding it the first time I read it. I never did forget it though.

What he said was, "You create as much pain in the world when you take offense as when you give offense."

I remember how offended I was when I first read that.

How in the world could he say such a thing? In my mind that concept seemed completely backwards. Isn't it those who give offense who cause all the pain and suffering in the world?

Well, now that I'm nearly three times that age I think I am a little bit wiser. Today I realize Yogananda was actually being quite gentle when he said that. The fact is you actually create *more* pain in the world when you take offense then when you give offense.

How is that possible?

It is because Yogananda was referring to your world, the one you perceive from your unique point of view. The only world this book refers to.

If someone gives you offense in your particular world they can in fact cause you some pain. But the pain they can cause you is microscopic compared to the pain you can cause yourself. They can cause you pain for a moment in time.

You, on the other hand, can create a living hell for yourself by taking that pain and focusing your attention on it for the rest of your life. Remember the library of videotapes we discussed in Chapter 14?

Taking offense is simply focusing attention on your pain by playing a negative tape over and over.

And the more you focus on your pain, the more pain you create for yourself.

So why would you create unnecessary pain for yourself? What could possibly motivate you?

What motivates you is your desire to be right.

There's a very wise saying you may have heard. That's saying is *"Would you rather be right or happy."*

Now you know what that saying means. Insisting on being right is insisting on not being happy. And it is entirely your choice.

Personally, I don't care if I'm right or wrong or if anybody else is right or wrong. I'm interested in being at peace, joyous, productive and happy. If that means I ignore somebody saying something offensive to me or accept rude service with a smile that is completely okay with me.

I see allowing another person to offend me as giving my control over to them. If someone else has the power to make me angry or upset than I am giving him or her control over my mind.

I don't do that anymore. I retain as much control as possible over my mind by controlling how I react to others' actions.

You must decide for yourself. Would you rather enjoy the emotional adrenaline rush you can give yourself into by being offended with all sorts of things that are happening around you: Or would you rather maintain control and stay in the calm center of your mind?

If you're having a hard time with this concept go back and reread Chapters 6 and 8.

Getting emotional over things is very exciting, stimulating and, in a bizarre way, fun.

Feeling self-righteous is very comforting. It certainly is nice to feel better than other people by getting offended by what they do.

Plus getting offended allows you the luxury of getting sympathy from your friends and relatives. It gives you all sorts of dramatic stories to talk about. You can tell them about how horrible and painful the experience was and they will offer sympathy and support.

I know because I used to prefer all of those things myself.

I loved being self-righteous. I could find things wrong with almost anybody. Nobody out there understood things as well as I did, nor did they do business as ethically as I did.

I really enjoyed telling my friends how other real estate agents, the folks at county planning and the government agencies wronged me. It felt so comforting to hear them agreeing with me.

So I do understand how tempting it is to continue to react to things the way you have been reacting to them as far back as you remember. I was there for close to five decades.

I finally changed when I realized how thinking like this was shooting myself in the foot.

There is no escaping the fact there are always going to be things we see as wrong in the outside world. And for some bizarre reason our minds are completely attracted to the wrong side of life.

Nevertheless, the truth is, forgiveness is a big key to enjoying every moment of your life.

And here is one way you can offer forgiveness every day in real life.

It's fairly easy to understand the concept of forgiveness but actually doing it can be quite a challenge.

Let me give you an accelerated version of a technique that's been taught for thousands of years to help deal with this issue of forgiveness.

Typical life situation: There's a bunch of items on your cell phone bill that you don't understand. So you call up and are put on hold for 20 minutes.

A voice in your mind starts screaming, "How the world can they do this to me." You keep listening to the stupid music they play, and you keep getting fooled when there's a break and an electronic voice says, "Your call is very important to us." Every time you focus on how long it is taking to answer a simple question you get angrier and angrier. You have dozens of things you need to do and this company is taking up all of your time. You are starting to feel so frustrated you could explode.

What can you possibly do to forgive in this situation?

While you are sitting there on hold ask yourself, "How can I use this dead time to forgive myself."

Then think of all the times you put somebody else off on the phone. All of the times you put someone on hold and forgot about him or her at work. All the times you didn't call your friend or relative back.

And instead of focusing on the frustration of being on hold, start telling yourself, "I forgive myself for not calling mom back. I forgive myself for leaving that poor guy on hold the other day. I forgive myself for not answering the phone when I saw it was a friend I didn't feel like speaking to..."

You get the idea. Continue to remember things connected with the telephone that you are uncomfortable with and use the current situation to forgive yourself for any similar situation you may feel guilty of.

By the time the customer service representative comes on the line to help you are going to feel completely forgiving towards him or her.

You can modify this technique to use in almost any situation.

Here is why it works.

All of the stuff we lash out at others about is based on things that we are holding inside ourselves.

In other words we accuse people of exactly the things we haven't forgiven ourselves for.

That may be uncomfortable for you to realize but it is the truth.

THE LIE OF BETRAYAL

At the practical level people should be able to make honest sense of betrayal and also to temper its consequences: to handle it, not be assaulted by it.

~ Rodger L. Jackson

While on the subject of forgiveness let's touch a real hot button issue – betrayal.

I personally just went through an experience that gave me the feeling that a good friend "betrayed" me.

So did he betray me, or did my feelings betray me?

My feelings.

No matter what my friend did – there was no betrayal involved.

There never is.

Hard to swallow but, in truth, no one ever "betrays" you. They betray your belief systems. *(See Chapter 7.)*

Much is made of the ultimate crime/sin of betrayal.

You hear endless chatter about how this person or that person betrayed someone's trust. Or how someone who was loyal to your particular opinion, team, social group, religion, politics etc. "betrayed" you and/or the cause.

So let's dig down under all the noise and see what betrayal actually is.

Betrayal happens when you entrust another with your beliefs.

I am not saying don't share your beliefs. I am asking you to understand beliefs are flexible and invite betrayal.

For example, at one point you probably believed in Santa Claus. Was it a betrayal to your parents, to yourself, your siblings, when you realized it was a myth? No. You just had new information.

All sorts of things can create this flexibility; more knowledge, as in the case of Santa; guilt, as when a friend is fooling around on another friend; and sometimes fear and intimidation.

To use an extreme example of the latter, consider the person who betrayed Jews in Germany during World War II: that person's fear for her own life, or, sadly, her buy in with the Nazi message of hate, became her personal belief system that led to the betrayal.

Rather than judge this person by saying she betrayed others, and thus mirror the same judgment that allows such events to occur, consider having compassion for her fear or lack of information.

By allowing compassion to be the antidote to judgment, by refusing to get on the judgment teeter-totter, your heart remains balanced and there ceases to be a "need" to betray or feel betrayed in order to assuage your own fear or lack of information. *(See graphic at the end of this chapter for more about "The Teeter-totter of Judgment.")*

The operative principle is: Beliefs are yours as you understand them and not necessarily as someone else does.

In short, betrayal is a response to a conflict in belief systems.

No more, no less.

It has nothing to do with sin, morals, trust or anything else. All those things, while juicy and exciting to talk about, are irrelevant to what betrayal actually is. Betrayal is another person having a different belief system than you have. They are acting on their own information and emotions.

Why is that a surprise?

Put another way, betrayal is simply proof that you are not the Supreme Commander of All Humans.

Why should that glaringly obvious fact be so hard to swallow?

Why should you or I be so devastated when it proves itself?

So next time you start to go into a rage because of the betrayal thing, get out your "Supreme Commander of All Humans" superhero suit, put it on and see how silly you look in it.

People are people. Everyone grows and learns at his or her own pace. Therefore, people make mistakes. They disappoint. They say the wrong things at the wrong times to the wrong people. In other words, they are just like you and me.

You can call it betrayal if you like.

Or you can exercise compassion, and thus find a way to forgive, forget, and enjoy yourself.

Like so much else, the choice is yours: anger or enjoyment.

I know which one I'd choose...

The Teeter-Totter of Judgment

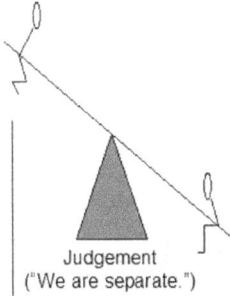

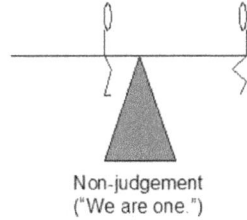

Judgement
("We are separate.")

Non-judgement
("We are one.")

Belief In Separation
aka Judgment

("I am different than the other person.")
This belief puts us at odds with the weight of the other person's emotions and we enter into a contest of wills where one person is always in a more precarious place than another.

Belief in Oneness
aka Non-Judgment
The closer we are to non-judgment (away from the idea of separation and being better than someone else) the less likely we are to be at the mercy of the other person's emotional weight. This allows us to avoid the feeling of helplessness. The closer we are to the center the more weight we have without effort of any kind. Guilt ceases to be an issue. Control ceases to be an issue. Balance naturally occurs.

Graphic by Jenifer Kay Hood

Chapter 17

Step 7: How To Grow Appreciation And Create Joy Feedback Loops

One joy scatters a hundred griefs.

- Chinese Proverb

WOULD you like to learn how to create some joy right this minute? Try this simple technique.

For most of our lives we are so involved in focusing on things we don't like that we rarely focus our energy on the things we appreciate.

Appreciation is simply another form of gratitude. In order to create an "avalanche of joy" we have to enhance the appreciative state of mind as much as possible.

Simply by doing this you can change the way you relate to the outside world on a regular basis.

Appreciation is something one has to grow. Consider it a plant that needs watering and attention to flourish.

I find the best seed to start this plant growing is to find something, anything, around you that you really appreciate no matter how insignificant.

After focusing on that for a while, you find something else you can add to your feeling of appreciation.

The additional things you appreciate become the water and fertilizer that helps the plant grow strong and healthy. The more you water it the bigger the appreciation plant gets.

This technique isn't difficult at all. Simply start by focusing on things you already appreciate easily.

Wherever you are keep an eye out for something to appreciate. Anything will do as long as it is something that you personally enjoy.

Perhaps your appreciation seed is a beautiful color on the wall or even the texture of the rug. Maybe yours is a well-dressed person; piece of jewelry; piece of art; beautiful music playing in the background or…

Focus on whatever you see as pleasant. Then appreciate and be grateful for it. Once you have done that, immediately find something else to appreciate and repeat the process.

Let me give you an example.

"I am really glad that the weather is nice enough to ride my bike today. I am so happy I found this great bike that is easy to ride. This sunshine feels fantastic on my skin. I love exercising like this; it is so invigorating. That person in the car is so nice to stop for me. Those magnolia trees smell incredible. I'm so lucky to live in this town where there are bike lanes."

Every time you notice and appreciate something you will automatically and effortlessly raise your vibration because you will start feeling joyous.

The longer you continue to do this appreciation focus the higher your joy vibration will rise.

This simple exercise can cause the world and circumstances around you to seem entirely different.

Here is why.

When you focus your attention on your problems and difficulties you are creating a vibration of conflict and drama. This is guaranteed to attract more conflict and drama into your life.

The universe is like the proverbial magic genie in a bottle. It will fulfill all of your wishes. But there is a catch.

The catch is how the universe determines what it is you desire. It makes its determination by looking at what percentage of time you occupy your mind with the desired outcome or object.

The universe believes that what you are thinking about the most is what you want more of in your life.

It makes sense if you look at it logically. After all, at any one moment in time there are a four million things we can choose to focus on - so obviously the thing we choose to focus on is our desire.

When we focus on how bad things are - we get more bad things coming into our life.

When we focus on drama and conflict - we get drama and conflict in our life –*and in spades.*

This is because the universe is so generous. The universe wants to give us more and more of what we desire.

For example, have you ever accidentally hit your thumb with a hammer and then began to concentrate so much on it that it seemed like every time you so much as moved you hit your sore thumb again?

Or how about a time when you were late to a meeting and as then as soon as you started worrying about traffic you managed to get stuck behind every slow driver, every stop sign, and every fender bender.

When this happens to me I quietly surrender to being late. "Oh, well," I tell myself. "I'll adjust to the way things are flowing right now. I'll just enjoy the scenery while I wait for this light" Then somehow the light changes, traffic seems to flow more easily, I find a closer parking space, and the person I was supposed to meet ends up later than I was!

This is what happens when the universe perceives that the majority of the time you are appreciating all the wonderful gifts offered to you every single day.

When the universe sees that you are no longer interested in drama or conflict it no longer throws people and circumstances at you in dramatic ways.

Simple rule: The longer you focus on it the more of it you will get.

When you focus on the positive, the universe starts presenting gifts and the people to your life in warm, friendly and loving ways. This is because the universe will offer you things that match your desires, which are all the beautiful and loving things you thank the universe for by appreciating them.

This exercise alone can make a dramatic difference in your life.

No psychotherapy, journeying, trances, soul retrieval or churches are necessary. No laying on a bed of nails required.

All that is required to employ this technique is a willingness to feel good.

How can something this simple be so powerful?

Because it works like this...

The problems disappear simply because you are no longer energizing them with your powerful thoughts. Any new difficulties that arrive are seen in their proper perspective, at most as minor irritations and hardly worth consideration at all when balanced against the beauty in the world.

Learn and practice this technique on a regular basis and something truly amazing will happen.

You'll start having days where absolutely everything goes completely right, like a perfect dream: no stress, no pain, no conflict, nothing but joy and happiness.

It is like the world starts cooperating with your every need and desire. You feel surrounded by love rather than tension and stress.

The more you do it the better it works. The better it works the more joyful your life gets.

Best of all, it is fun and easy.

JOY FEEDBACK LOOPS

Count your joys instead of your woes; count your friends instead of your foes.

~ Irish proverb

Let me start by defining "positive feedback loop."

The Archeology Dictionary defines feedback loop in this way: A system's response to external stimuli leading to further changes that serve to reinforce the initial response, thereby creating and accelerating a cause and effect loop.

A joy feedback loop uses your system's response (by responding with joyous thoughts) to external stimuli (the outside world) leading to further changes that serve to reinforce the initial response (creating even more joyful thoughts).

Here is where I hand the reins over to you.

To create joy feedback loops it's going to be your task to find the things that create joy in your life. You have already learned many places to start this process. I told you some of the ways I've used and given starting points for you to create your own.

In order for you to create joy feedback loops what brings me joy is absolutely irrelevant. The only thing that matters is what makes you feel happy, joyous, and alive.

In Chapter 1, I said you were the most uniquely interesting person who has ever existed in the history of mankind.

And part of what makes you so interesting is that what excites me may bore you.

When I look at the vast kaleidoscope of delightful people out there I embrace the fact that each and every one of them is completely different from me. We all have completely different wants, desires, needs, motivation and yes, even religious and spiritual beliefs.

If we didn't all believe and feel differently about life we would be a stagnant and dead society. Instead we are a vibrant and evolving people.

To create joy feedback loops you need to search within your heart and find out exactly what brings *you* joy. Don't worry about the big things that bring you joy. Watch for all the small, seemingly insignificant things that bring a smile to your face and a happy feeling to your heart.

For each of us those things are different. And lots of these things may seem "silly" to your friends and family. That's okay. They may not understand today. But they will someday. And if they never do that is because they are themselves unique human beings with their own set of joy makers.

To help you discover your own, here are some examples of what I use to create my personal joy feedback loops.

For me singing opens up my heart. I sing in the shower. I sing while I do my chores and work. I even sing when I'm walking down the street. It makes me feel very happy. Occasionally I'll get a strange look, but more often I get knowing smiles.

Petting and playing with my silly, lovable, and polydactyl cat, Frankie.

Remembering my beautiful hikes in the Oregon woods.

Playing back some of the beautiful sunsets I have seen at the coast.

Looking in the faces of very young babies and children when I am out and about.

Watching young people in love holding hands and showing affection.

Sitting on a bench in the park and taking a break for a few minutes to watch the river flow by.

Walking to the toy department and seeing all the cool toys that didn't exist when I was young.

Remembering the soothing sound of my mother singing, "Itsy-bitsy spider" to me when I was just a child.

Watching my beautiful sister Kate on television diving off the high board in competition when I was about nine.

Appreciating my brother Joseph's incredible sculptures depicting endangered species.

The feeling of relief and gratitude when my sister Barbara pulled me out of a pool and saved me from drowning when I was about eight years old. I've always felt that my life since that day was a gift.

Now it's your turn.

We all have this vast bank of incredibly beautiful memories to choose from. Start exploring them. Look for the ones that really make you feel fantastic. And when you find one, remember it. Make a note so you can bring it back at will.

There is certainly no harm in running pleasurable memories over and over again. You certainly have done it enough with the unpleasant memories.

A CAUTIONARY NOTE

In the beginning of your quest for *Unstoppable Joy* it is best to avoid contact with a lot of the "normal" activities of society that can easily pull you into a negative feedback loop. I am talking about critical people, the news, most radio, and unfortunately, most television shows.

These things will bring up the most horrible images imaginable. They can be very detrimental to trying to maintain a positive feedback loop.

I see no benefit in focusing your mental energy on thinking about some war on the other side of the world or some newly discovered disease when you could think about things that will make you joyous, healthy and productive.

Of course, I am not saying you avoid all issues. If it's something you can do something about, of course do something about it. But if it's something that you have no personal power over at this moment there is little benefit to focusing your attention on it.

HARNESS JOY POWER BY PAMPERING YOURSELF

When we care for ourselves we care for others.

--Anonymous

Treating yourself well is a very important step in the path to joy and is another way to create joy feedback loops.

It seems like all of us would tend to do this naturally, but most of us seem to put doing nice things for ourselves last on the list of importance.

In fact, it is amazing how rough we treat ourselves overall. We live in a society where virtually every word or phrase is work related. We prioritize, we analyze, we delegate, we do tasks, we make lists, we schedule, we carry cell phones, Blackberries, laptop computers, iPods, Palm pilots, and on and on.

We keep ourselves ready to work and communicate at the first bell, email or buzzer that catches our attention.

While all of these gizmos and communication devices might be nice they have very little to do with treating yourself well.

As I have explained, we seem to have gotten very far away from simply pampering ourselves and enjoying the moment in this society. That ugly fact is a very big reason why so many of us have found joy slipping away like a memory of the distant past.

Your incredible body is the most amazing vehicle ever constructed. It can do tons of work. It can stay up endless hours. If you tell it to it will continue to work until you have given it a raging headache and all of its muscles are completely exhausted.

It is the humblest and most obedient servant imaginable. You tell it what to do and it does it. It rarely asks you questions about whether the orders you are giving it are wise or in its best interest. It simply obeys and followed your directions, no matter how absurd they are.

You can tell it to run and play, which it would love; or you can force to sit in a chair for 12 hours straight, which it would hate. It only complains when you have worked it so hard that it has no choice but to start hurting and giving you pain feedback for its own survival.

Start looking at your body more as a loyal servant rather than as "you," because in truth you are not your body. You are the energy powering the body.

Your body is very aware of how you treat it. That is why it feels so wonderful when you slip into a hot tub or get a massage. It rewards you with wonderful feelings when you give it even the slightest pampering. Those feelings are your body talking to you. It is saying, "Thank you... this feels so good. I really deserve this."

And you really *do* deserve it. In my opinion, you deserve a treat far more often than you tend to give yourself one.

How can you expect to have an appreciation for all the wonderful experiences and feelings this life has to offer if you deprive your body of the pleasure and relaxation it wants to experience?

I cannot over emphasize the importance of this step. To be joyous you must give your body joy on a regular basis.

Every time your body signals that what you are doing feels good and pleasurable make a note. Put that on the list of things you want to do regularly.

Here are a few questions for you to ponder.

When was the last time you soaked for 20 minutes in a hot bathtub and allowed yourself to simply relax and enjoy it? How often would be too often to take a bath like this?

When was the last time you went out and gave your body a nice relaxing massage? How often do you feel would be too often?

When was the last time you soaked your body in scented oil and Epsom salts?

Or even sat quietly in your living room with no television, music, telephone, or computer, putting your energy towards calming your body and relaxing your mind?

When was the last time you laid on the grass in the park or on your lawn simply enjoying the blissful feeling of sunshine bathing and caressing your body?

Or sat simply staring at the moon and stars?

I give myself these pleasures several times a week.

If you really want a life of joy those sorts of activities are not optional. They are required.

In case you don't see why this is so important consider the research by the Touch Research Institute at the University of Miami:

> The Touch Research Institute has conducted over 100 studies on the positive effects of massage therapy on many functions and medical conditions in many different age groups. Among the significant research findings are enhanced growth (e.g. in preterm infants), diminished pain (e.g. fibromyalgia), decreased autoimmune problems (e.g., increased pulmonary function in asthma and decreased glucose levels in diabetes), enhanced

immune function (e.g., increased natural killer cells in HIV and cancer), and enhanced alertness and performance (e.g., EEG pattern of alertness and better performance on math computations). Many of these effects appear to be mediated by decreased stress hormones.

How bad do you want a life of joy? Are you willing to do what is necessary?

Do you think you have the willpower to actually treat yourself well?

In our society most such activities are considered to be a waste of time.

I don't consider them a waste of time. I consider them to be "a taste of time." As in savoring the delectable taste of this moment in time.

Why is it most of us treat our bodies so poorly? Where did we get the idea that pushing ourselves so hard was in our own best interest?

I've known many people who treated their bodies like slaves all of their lives. Constantly beating them and pushing them until the bodies were in absolute stress and exhaustion.

The end result was always the same. At one point the body would get a horrible illness or perhaps a heart attack or a stroke. It would cry, "Stop this... I can't take it anymore. If you won't stop voluntarily, I'll make you stop!"

And so it stops; sometimes permanently, all because the owner of the body never gave it the pampering it needed so badly.

So take note. If you haven't been listening to the messages your body gives you... perhaps you should listen to this advice from a stranger.

As you treat your body so your body will treat you.

Feed it a regular diet of joy and it will return all that joy with interest.

Feed it a diet of stress and abuse and it will return all the stress and abuse with greater interest.

In both cases the interest we are talking about here is compounded daily. The longer you feed it either of those diets, the more dramatic the payoff will be.

CHAPTER 18

STEP 8: FIND ADVENTURE IN EVERYDAY CHALLENGES

The biggest adventure you can take is to live the life of your dreams.

~ Oprah Winfrey

S O far this book has taught you a few basic principles necessary to create a life of joy. Before I continue I will briefly recap a few of the highlights.

When you begin living in joy you will be able to control what manifests in all aspects of your everyday life.

When you realize that every day is a gift, and that no matter how bad things seem it's far better than the alternative, you can start looking at life as an adventure rather than a trial.

If you're in control of your responses when extremely challenging things happen you can keep them in perspective.

When you take time to create joy feedback loops, accentuate the positive and pamper yourself even the worst day can be better.

Finally, and most relevant to this step, is the acknowledgement that life can be an adventure or an absolutely terrifying trial depending on what you choose to focus on.

We all face challenges. Some of them can be overwhelming. But as with everything else in life we get to choose how we look at it. The challenge itself has no power to make us see things one way or the other. Luckily, we get to choose how we look at things.

I'm going to use a real simple analogy here to help explain this concept.

For those of you that have been to Disneyland you will remember the Jungle Cruise ride in Adventureland.

If you haven't been there you most likely have heard of it. It was one of the original rides and has been entertaining people for 50 years.

In the Jungle Cruise ride you step into a boat and cruise the waters of an actual river that was created at Disneyland. You float off around the bend and you are in the middle of the jungle with life size, animated models of animals that are quite realistic looking. You go through herds of elephants, swarms of crocodiles, get charged by a wild rhino, menaced by hungry tigers and nearly have the boat capsized by hippopotamus.

After being entertained for 15 minutes or so you arrive safely back at the port.

Those of us who maintain a joyful outlook experience the challenges in our lives in much the same way as passengers experience the Jungle Cruise.

Important point: the Jungle Cruise is only fun because you "think" you're in control of the situation.

If you didn't think you were in control, the experience would be horrific. You would not arrive at the end of the journey laughing and smiling. Instead your heart would be pounding, you would be covered in sweat, and very, very thankful to be alive.

Think about it. If you believed the hippopotamus could actually capsize that boat and leave you in the river with man-eating crocodiles the cruise wouldn't seem like a whole lot of fun. If you actually believed that those tigers might have leaped on board the boat and started ripping peoples' throats out, you certainly wouldn't have feelings of delight.

No: the only reason you are able to enjoy it is because you are operating under the belief system that you are entirely safe because you are in a controlled situation. You believe there was no possibility of anything going wrong.

Because of that you saw the experience as a joyous adventure.

Interested in knowing the truth about the Jungle Cruise? You are probably no safer on the jungle ride than you are in the jungle itself.

In truth, according to the U.S. Consumer Product Safety Commission, 4.5 people per year in America die in amusement parks and in 2005 there were more than 15,000 amusement ride-related injuries in the U.S.

You could have been seriously injured. You could have died. It happens. The statistics prove it.

So much for the belief system that you were in a completely safe and controlled situation...

The secret is that *you believed you were safe.* The firm belief that you were safe was what allowed you to enjoy the ride so much.

I have news for you: you are in no more danger in your everyday life than on the jungle ride.

So why not enjoy the adventures of every day life with the same happiness and joy you face the lions and tigers on the Jungle Cruise?

When the rhinoceros of a doctors' grim diagnosis starts charging you, when the hungry crocodiles of debt surround you, when a change in your job situation, the stock market or the real estate market rears up like a hippopotamus to capsize your boat, remember... this is all a joyous adventure!

No matter how scary all of these things look, the overwhelming likelihood is that you're going to arrive back at the port in total safety.

You have faced major challenges before in your life. Losing a job or loved one, surviving a car crash, doing badly on a test... One way or another they all work out: every single time. That's why you are able to sit here safely reading this book.

What makes you think the next challenge is going to be any different than the last ones?

I repeat: Today's challenges are all going to work out. You have the experience of the past to prove it.

Those of us who stay in a state of joy understand that everything is going to be okay. We know that no matter how sinister those tigers look, how hungry those crocodiles look, or how fast that hippopotamus seems to be charging at us that one way or another it is all going to work out.

So we hang onto our seats and watch the ride with a smile.

We also make sure that we squeeze out every bit of enjoyment we possibly can while we are overcoming these challenges.

It is the challenges that make this life such an adventure.

So hold on, smile and enjoy the ride!

CHAPTER 19

STEP 9: NEVER UNDERESTIMATE THE POWER OF YOUR WORDS

"We cannot always control our thoughts, but we can control our words, and repetition impresses the subconscious, and we are then master of the situation."

~ Florence Scovel Shinn

ONE of the trickier parts of enabling a life of joy is gaining control over the words you are saying.

A survey by the California Task Force for Social Responsibility determined that 80% of people are hurt by words and that only 20% of children and adults are able to handle put downs without emotional pain or psychological damage.

Think of what affect that has on a global scale!

Now consider how harmful the belief system is that says our words are not really all that important.

Much of this belief system stems from times in childhood when we heard our parents, brothers and sisters say things like, "I'd love to kill that person," or "I really hate that person," or even such things as, "I hate my life," or "Things are always going to be difficult for us."

The mind of a child is quite sophisticated. We hear those around us make statements like that yet inside ourselves we know they are not really true. So our sophisticated yet childish minds decide that the words these people are saying unimportant because they don't reflect how the people really feel.

This has even more impact when one considers a study by Jack Canfield. It showed that children hear 432 negative versus 32 positive words a day!

As children we don't understand why those around us would say things they don't really stand behind 100%. Since we see it happening all around us we start doing it ourselves because we want to be accepted.

So when we didn't get exactly the present we wanted for our birthday and our friends ask us how our birthday was we respond with, " I hated my birthday. I didn't get what I want."

When in truth we actually had a great time on our birthday.

Or when our parents ask us what we think of the teacher we respond with, "I don't like that teacher." In fact, she only did something to irritate us that day. In the overall picture, we actually like that teacher a lot.

But we are okay with saying those things because we learn from those around us that the words one uses are not really all that important. After all, we reason, actions speak louder than words, right?

As we get older we learn the destructive habit of gossip. We learn how to talk behind people's backs and how to judge others in school. All of our friends have tons of people they like to make judgments about as well.

In the end we all support each other in this. So it is yet another insincere and self-destructive habit we learn so those around us will accept us.

This attitude of words not being important is even common in mundane everyday conversation. How many times have you asked someone if they were hungry and had them answer, "I'm starving"?

In fact, they are nowhere close to starving; and probably have never experienced starvation in their life.

Yet, since "words aren't important," we say we're starving.

It seems as if the more we get caught up in talking the less aware we are of the feelings going on inside ourselves.

Here is one of the biggest steps to existing in joy. Start becoming aware of the feelings that exist inside you when you say certain things.

As much as you possibly can, start carefully monitoring what you say (which is a challenge in its own).

Then, as you are doing this, start noticing the feelings you get while you are talking about certain subjects or expressing yourself to people.

The results of this simple mental discipline can be quite astonishing.

You will find that subjects you talk about all the time can easily sap you of all of your joy.

GOSSIP

Whoever gossips to you will gossip about you.

~ Spanish Proverb

A fantastic example of how words can sap you of joy is gossip. Gossip never makes you feel happy or joyous. By its nature it simply can't.

Gossip is so distasteful that a recent survey by Ranstad staffing showed 60% of people cited gossip as the #1 problem in the workplace.

Since we can't see the big picture anything we say about anyone else is based completely on judgment and conjecture. Whether it is a coworker or Paris Hilton anything we say about them in the line of gossip is going to make us feel bad about ourselves.

This is because down deep we know that we don't have all of the facts concerning another person's life.

The more you gossip the sicker you are going to feel inside. Sure you may get a temporary rush from the laughter of your friends for your clever comments, but deep down inside you are not going to feel good about yourself.

So why do we do it? Why do we talk about things that make us feel bad?

Is it in our best interest to do so? I don't think so.

Most criticism we dole out at others falls under the same category. It may feel superficially good to criticize a person, but inside we are not really going to feel good about it at all.

How many times in your life have you finally gotten the opportunity to "tell that person off" and an hour or later felt awful about it?

You may have even thought to yourself, "I wish I hadn't even bothered." The reason you thought that is because it didn't feel good.

COMPLAINING

You can complain because roses have thorns, Or you can rejoice because thorns have roses.

—Tom Wilson

Now I'll throw the big one at you. Complaining.

Where in the world did we get this absurd idea that complaining about anything is going to do anything but make us feel bad?

Yet we see it and hear it everywhere! I can't even begin to enumerate the amount of things I hear people complain about every day—everything from politics to the weather and a thousand subjects in between.

Next time you start complaining about something tune into your feelings. Complaining and joy do not go together. They are like fire and water.

Complaining is one of the easiest ways to kill joy ever invented by human beings.

Yet we seem to love to do it. Some folks complain almost all the time.

And we get back to my basic question.

Is it in your best interest to say words that make you feel bad inside?

If not, why do you continue to do it?

Okay, I can hear you all saying, "Ed, what in the world are we supposed to talk about? Does everything we talk about make us feel bad?"

No, not at all.

There are many subjects you can talk about that will increase your joy. Some will increase your joy to the point where you are about to explode with it.

A great one is encouragement. Goethe once said, "Correction does much, encouragement does more." Try using encouraging words with someone and tune into those feelings inside of yourself. You might be amazed at how wonderful it feels.

Compliments are really nice as well. I make a point of complimenting virtually everyone I come face-to-face with. There is always something nice you can say about someone. It can be as simple is how they have styled their hair, the wonderful jewelry they're wearing, their carefully coordinated clothes, or even their beaming smile.

Everyone has something worth complimenting.

Go out and give a compliment today. Then tune into those feelings inside.

You will find joy bubbling up every time you compliment someone.

The more you do it the more joyous you are going to feel.

Is it in your best interest to say things that make you feel joyous? To me, the answer is obvious.

AN EXPERIMENT

Let yourself be silently drawn by the stronger pull of what you love.

--Rumi

Try this as an experiment. Next time you are with a group of your friends who are gossiping and complaining start talking about the wonderful things that have happened in your life.

Most likely you will immediately run into some resistance. As you continue to do it though you will notice something amazing starts to happen.

Not only will you feel joyous inside yourself, the conversation will start turning to wonderful things that have happened in their lives as well. This is because actually people would rather feel joyous than destructive.

Give folks a chance to feel joyous and most of the time they will take it.

So by doing this little experiment you have not only brought yourself joy, you are spreading it around to others.

Every time you talk about wonderful things you are watering the seeds of joy that live within you.

Even the simplest things count. The beautiful sunshine, the wonderful smell of the roses, the blossoming trees, wonderful music, an inspiring speech you heard, or any of a million other things can be used to create joy all around you by simply using your mouth and tongue.

It's your choice: you can either talk about joyful things or destructive things.

But when making that choice remember: every word you say is adding to your own personal joy or subtracting from it. So choose your words wisely and watch your joy grow.

THINK FIRST, TALK LATER

"A careless word may kindle strife,

A cruel word may wreck a life,

A timely word may lessen stress,

A loving word may heal and bless."

-- Author Unknown

Now you know why I believe words are important. But you may be asking yourself, "Does this mean I can't express my feelings?"

The answer is, no.

What it does mean is you should think first, talk later.

There is a reason why seasoned diplomats pause before answering a question. They know that the wrong word in a different culture can literally make all the difference in the world.

A classic example of this is the mistake Chevrolet made in naming a model Nova." They wondered, "Why aren't Spanish speakers buying this new model?" Because in Spanish "No va" means it doesn't go, so potential Hispanic buyers thought the car wouldn't run properly.

These days when a car is named there is a whole army of people making sure the name of the model is language neutral—or changed in a country that might misunderstand the model name's meaning.

How does this apply when you are faced with personal dissatisfaction?

An example:

Say your wife gives you a sweater. It fits but you dislike the color or pattern.

You could take it with a smile and then stuff it into a Goodwill box at the first opportunity.

You could say, "Thanks, but I think I'd like something else," thus deflating the person's desire to please.

Or you could stop a moment and think about how you could say it in a way that gets your point across without diminishing the other person's attempt to please you. How about, "Thanks so much. It's great having a sweater that fits but I don't think this pattern suits me. Would you be terribly hurt if I exchanged it?"

Approaching it this way you have done four important things.

1. You have genuinely thanked the person.
2. You have acknowledged what was right about their choice.
3. You have explained your position by taking responsibility for your own reaction.
4. You have attempted to protect the other person's feelings.

Can you think of a time when such a reaction would have made a family celebration more fun?

I can.

Would practicing this sort of diplomacy protect your self-interest?

Most likely.

This method also applies when faced with much more serious breaches of confidence or trust.

By expressing yourself in a way that protects your self-interest, taking responsibility for your own reaction and respecting the other person's reality you are able to model joyous living.

Think of how this would help others reflect joy back to you...then remember how that protects everyone's self-interest.

So next time someone does something that you find displeasing take a moment to remind yourself to, "Think first, talk later." Your reward is a more joyous, more balanced relationship with that person—and with yourself.

CHAPTER 20

STEP 10: SHARE YOUR JOY AND HAPPINESS WITH EVERYONE

False happiness renders men stern and proud, and that happiness is never communicated. True happiness renders them kind and sensible, and that happiness is always shared.

~ Charles de Montesquieu

THE wonderful thing about joy is how contagious it is. When you start talking about wonderful things that have happened in your life you will find all those around you smiling and feeling better. Of course, on the other hand, when you start talking about things that are miserable those around you will catch that misery. In the worst cases, they will chime in and start telling you about their misery.

Then we have created a "pity party."

We have all been in those conversations where people spend all night comparing financial or health problems. It literally can become a contest of who is the most miserable.

I am happy to lose those contests.

In fact, if I can avoid it, I no longer participate in those sorts of conversations and suggest you avoid them as well.

What I like to do instead is tell people how wonderful things are in my life. Then all of a sudden they'll remember wonderful things in their lives and start talking about them. Pretty soon there is a whole mass of positive energy flowing around.

The sharing of joyousness is far more important than you may realize in maintaining your own state of joy.

Sharing your joy is an amplification of the Golden Rule: "Do unto others as you would have them do unto you."

By offering joy to others you will find that others offer joy to you.

But it goes much deeper than this. When you share joy with others you are reinforcing all of your personal feelings of joy. You are validating the truth of joy.

Plus you are benefiting those you offer your joy to. You are raising their vibration to a much higher level. By doing so you simply cannot help but raise your own vibration.

It's easy to do but it is hard to remember. Unfortunately, in our society most conversations tend to go to the dark side. People seem to love to talk about illnesses, financial problems, and disasters.

So you may feel just a bit like the Lone Ranger by bringing a positive slant into the social situation. Some folks may even give you strange looks and not participate in the joyous conversation. They may simply be so comfortable in their state of victimhood that getting out of it could be difficult.

Of course over time this will change. After awhile people will expect joy from you and you will find yourself being welcomed in virtually every social and business situation.

Why? Because people prefer to feel good. And when they connect those good feelings with you, you will find yourself welcomed with open arms.

In other words, once folks become used to the new, positive version of you that is what they will expect from you.

Which will make you even more positive and joyous because we tend to rise to folks' expectations of us.

The sharing of joy is so important that it is the reason I am writing this book. Over the past ten plus years I have discovered that the more I share joy, the more joy comes into my life.

So I want to share it with as many people as possible because sharing joy is *definitely* in my best interest.

CHAPTER 21

STEP 11: MAKE FRIENDS WITH WONDERFUL MR. DEATH

When we finally know we are dying, and all other sentient beings are dying with us, we start to have a burning, almost heartbreaking sense of the fragility and preciousness of each moment and each being, and from this can grow a deep, clear, limitless compassion for all beings.

- Sogyal Rinpoche:

I have some bad news for you. You have a terminal illness. There is no way around it. You'll just have to live with it. The name of the illness is "birth."

It's so sad. In every single recorded case everyone afflicted with the disease called birth will die.

That is the truth. Can you deal with it?

Many folks seem to have a big problem dealing with it – that is for sure.

We live in a society where people are overwhelmed by the fear of death.

Every direction you look you can see blatant evidence of this.

Just flip through a magazine or switch on the news and you are faced with a litany of advertisements that cater to the fear of death. Most of these come to us courtesy of pharmaceutical companies, all well aware that the average person will pay any amount of money to keep Mr. Death at bay. (As a reminder, see *Chapter 9*.)

I am continuously amazed at how far folks will go to keep the "death" part of reality away from their consciousness.

Human beings are a very strange lot. When someone is born we celebrate for a few days and then once a year until a person dies or gets so old we wonder if the person wants to be reminded of being alive. Then, when someone dies, it is considered normal to spend days, weeks, even years in mourning.

Yet birth and death are two sides of the same coin: Life.

To create a life of joy you must learn to look Mr. Death straight in the eyes. His appearance is as inevitable as sunset. The truth of the matter is, "no one gets out of here alive." Eventually, the crocodile of time is going to catch up with you. There is no way around that.

If you can't handle the inevitable fact you're going to die, you're going to have a hard time enjoying your wonderful time on this planet.

In my opinion, ignoring the fact you're going to leave here some day is the ultimate form of denial.

Personally, I look at Mr. Death as a wonderful friend. He's my best buddy. He's always at my shoulder.

Sure he may look a bit grim: skull for a head, dressed in a hooded, dark cloak and carrying his scythe.

Yet once you get over his personal appearance you start to realize what a great guy he is. He performs a wonderful function.

Because no matter how much I hang out with him he won't tell me when he is going to do his business. I can beg and cajole and he keeps his bony lips sealed.

Which is why I consider him so wonderful: because this uncertainty allows me to enjoy my life all the more.

Moment by moment he reminds me this might be my last day, my last hour, even perhaps my last five minutes. For that matter, maybe my last second...

So his message to me is loud and clear. His grim silence is telling me "You better make darn well sure you are enjoying every single moment you are alive."

When I am tempted to get angry, when I am tempted to go into misery, when I feel like life is simply overwhelming... I remind myself of the specter of wonderful Mr. Death.

I envision his grim countenance sitting right at my shoulder patiently waiting. I see him glancing down at the stopwatch he carries just for me. And I wonder when the buzzer will go off.

That's all I need to do to jolt my mind back to the reality that every single second here is a wonderful gift destined to disappear at any time.

I can take those remaining seconds and waste them by being angry. I could spin those remaining seconds into days, weeks or even years of misery.

Or I can come to my senses and realize how unimportant being angry, miserable or overwhelmed really is.

Once I come to my senses I thank Mr. Death. I acknowledge the wonderful service he provides by keeping me aware of my mortality.

So, when you think of death, don't be fearful. You have no choice in the matter of when, where and why Mr. Death finally does his business.

But until that moment you have all of the choices in the world.

Use them wisely.

CHAPTER 22

STEP 12: TAKE RESPONSIBILITY FOR YOUR OWN JOY AND SORROW

One can make a day any size and regulate the rising and setting of his own sun and the brightness of its shining.

~ John Muir

I have alluded to this fact throughout the book, so now I will simply state it. No matter what you may think or logic out about what caused you to be where you are right now, the truth is this…
You are here because of your thoughts, attitudes, fears, and actions.

You have created every aspect of the situation you now find yourself in.

No one else is responsible for where you are today, at this moment. Only you.

It isn't because of a bad childhood. It isn't because of an abusive spouse. It isn't because of poor upbringing or poverty or physical limitations or any of the other thousands of crutches we like to dwell upon and "blame."

Using these as excuses is deluding one's self. Big time. And a deluded mind cannot manifest *Unstoppable Joy*.

Before creating your new reality, you *must* take 100% responsibility for where you are today, at this very moment.

And this very moment has nothing to do with anything in your past or future. It has only to do with responsibility for where you are **right now**.

Without that vital mindset no amount of visualizing joy and prosperity, repeating affirmations or praying to God can make any difference.

Why? Because you are not honestly seeing what makes the present reality.

The truth is that we bring forth in life exactly what we focus our thoughts and actions on.

The Law of Perception and *Unstoppable Joy* are all about creating a new world for your self.

In this new world you'll find happiness, abundance, beauty, fulfillment and joy. It's a world of perfect health; a world of great relationships.

Those concepts are easy to swallow. We all want to live in that world. The question is: are you ready to take these lessons seriously and integrate them into your daily life. If the answer is yes, if you choose to act in your best interest, then that world can be yours starting today, **right now**.

The movies *What the Bleep Do We Know* and *The Secret* and many other books, tapes and belief systems going back thousands of years teach these same profound truths of how to create a new life.

But some of them skip this next ugly and necessary fact.

You cannot create this wonderful world from your thoughts until you realize you have created your *present* situation from your thoughts!

Without understanding this simple fact, without acknowledging that your thoughts and belief systems have created the reality of this very moment, you simply cannot create a new one for yourself.

Furthermore, if you cannot fully accept that your old thoughts and actions were used to create your present reality, there is absolutely no way you will be able to believe that using new thoughts and actions can create a new reality.

Here is an analogy to help you visualize what I am trying to get across:

You probably think your powerful thoughts have been like water - simply washing over you without having an effect.

In reality, they have been like paint; vividly coloring your present existence.

Many of us have used our thoughts, words and actions to paint ourselves into an unhappy corner.

Attempting to manifest a new reality with the belief that you aren't responsible for everything in your life is like trying to paint your house with water instead of paint.

Without understanding that only paint will leave a lasting impression, it wouldn't matter how many years you spent brushing water on your house.

You would still have the original color when you were finished.

So realize that your life is colored the way it is right now because of your actions and thoughts. Then it is a simple and logical progression to simply change those thoughts and actions to see the color of your life change in front of your eyes.

Whenever you are facing a challenge in life and your inner self asks, "Who or what is to blame for this?" do yourself a favor. Check out your brush to see if you're still painting with water. Are you covering the situation in dark thoughts thinking they have no effect?

If you are you'll know who is really to blame.

Then have a good, deep laugh and choose to paint in colors that suit your best interests.

CHAPTER 23

THE BIG CATCH

We are caught in an inescapable network of mutuality, tied in a single garment of destiny. Whatever affects one directly, affects all indirectly.

~ Martin Luther King, Jr.

THERE is a big catch to all of this.

It is a very scary and powerful truth they didn't teach in school.

"What you wish for others is what you will receive"

I call that truth, "The Catch."

Again, "what you wish for others is what you will receive. "

Why?

Because at a very deep level each and every limitation you desire for another human being is actually a limitation you are putting on yourself.

To put it in an even more bluntly: There is an excellent possibility the universe will give you the *worst possible thing* that you wish for others.

Like it or not.

This is the catch that keeps people from realizing the joy and prosperity they seek.

I have folks who come to me and say, "Ed, I have been following the exercises in *The Secret* for quite a while, but I don't seem to be manifesting a happier or better life for myself."

And I smile and tell them that actually the movie should have been called "*a* secret." It is part of the picture, but certainly not the whole thing.

This is because the great manifestations you want in life are primarily blocked by your own frames of reference and belief systems.

The biggest impediment is judgment.

The mechanics behind the way judgment blocks out joy and abundance are quite simple and straightforward.

It works like this: the filters you use in judging everyone else are the filters that will be applied to your joy and prosperity.

Let me give you an example in the simplest form.

Suppose you're talking with some friends about Paris Hilton. And everybody jokes and laughs about her life. Someone will likely make a comment of how it's so ridiculous that she can be so wealthy without apparently doing anything besides being famous. *(See Chapter 19 for more about using words.)*

You may even join in and gripe about how unfair it is that she can get so much money for doing so little work.

Your casual conversation with your powerful words has just given the universe a very important message. That message is that you don't feel you deserve to get money without doing a whole lot of hard work. You have just used judgment to put a creative wish in motion with your powerful mind.

By judging Paris' prosperity as undeserved you have told the universe you feel it is bad to receive money for doing virtually nothing.

The universe will be happy to comply with your wish by making sure you never win the lottery or easily and freely receive large sums of money. The universe is not about to give you something that you feel is "bad" for another.

The reason judgment works this way is the universe doesn't see any difference in any of us. The universe loves us all unconditionally. The universe doesn't judge. To the universe we are all her beloved children and we are all equal.

As partial payment for the precious miracle of life, the universe desires for you to look at people the same way the universe does. After all, you and millions of others were given the gift of life for free.

Because the gift of life is given equally to all, the dreams and wishes of each and every individual have equal weight.

Because of that fact the universe may well give you the worst possible thing you wish for another person.

You don't have to believe me.

If you want to see things differently that's okay. It is your choice. But don't expect to manifest lots of joy and beautiful things in your life.

The universe gives you complete freedom to play and create any sort of world that you want.

Some belief systems call this "free will." But most belief systems have the definition of free will completely wrong.

Free will is usually misinterpreted as meaning the freedom to sin or not to sin. That is not how this philosopher sees it.

I believe free will is actually the freedom to choose between living in heaven or living in hell while one is on this planet.

A big part of whether we choose heaven or hell has to do with how we judge others and judge the circumstances in our life.

Our thoughts towards others play a big part in creating either a life of *Unstoppable Joy* or Unrelenting Misery.

It's all about perception, folks. We decide where we put our focus. Nothing in the world around us is being forced upon us.

Everything is our choice.

We can look at the world through rose-colored glasses or we can look at the world through brown-colored glasses. We choose which pair we will wear at every moment, no one else.

Personally, I gave up my brown-colored glasses a while ago.

CHAPTER 24

THE BUFFET
OF EVERYDAY LIFE

Life is a banquet, but most poor suckers are starving to death.

–*Mame Dennis*

IN closing I will share a wonderful story. When it was told to me the first time it shook my entire belief system because it made so much sense.

Imagine the most beautiful and extravagant all-you-can-eat buffet you've ever seen. This buffet has every type of food imaginable from every country all over the world.

There are millions of people eating at this buffet. In spite of that, you can see that the line to get what you want is actually not very long at all.

So you enter this incredible Buffet of Life. There are literally thousands of choices of different types of food you can eat and desserts and drinks you can enjoy.

You grab your plate and get in line with all the other interesting folks. As you go down the line you are attracted to only the types of food you prefer. When you see something you enjoy you reach for it and put it on your plate.

You have now gone through the entire buffet and your plate is full with all of the foods that you like.

You think to yourself, "How wonderful it is to be in this amazing place where I can choose exactly what pleases me."

Then you take your plate to a table. You savor all of the wonderful variety of textures, colors, smells and flavors that attract you to your favorite foods. You then focus all of your energy into savoring the infinite delight of this delicious meal.

Too bad most of us don't live our lives like that at all.

Instead, after we choose what we desire, we walk around to all of the rest of the tables and look at what everyone else chose.

Then we start complaining about the choices that other people made.

We say, " Oh, my goodness, look at this person: he is eating pork. Pork is so horribly bad for you. Can you believe this person is eating pork? I hate pork!"

Then we stroll by another table and burst out with, "This person is having a big piece of cake. Cake is so fattening and expensive. I just find it horrible that this person is eating cake. Lots of people in the world can't even afford cake. Don't you all agree with me that it is awful for someone to eat cake?"

"And look, these people are eating Chinese food. Chinese food sucks. I don't like the way it tastes or looks. How could anyone eat that? Oh, jeez, this guy over here is eating hominy grits. That is gross. I don't know why that person is drinking Pepsi when everyone knows Coke is better."

If you actually acted that way in a buffet not only with those around you think you are extremely childish and rude, you would most likely be unceremoniously thrown out on your ear.

However, when you act that way in life, you are not thrown off the planet. If it worked that way this would be a lonely place.

But you *are* thrown out of Joy.

This profound analogy may help you to see that most of us act rude and childish at the Buffet of Life every single day.

On and on we go, day after day, year after year, criticizing, complaining, gossiping, hurting, judging, bitching and moaning and pointing our fingers at everyone else.

We could focus our energy on the things we desire and find wonderful on this planet. We could utilize our powerful minds to create more of the things we enjoy and by doing so bring more joy to everyone else in the world.

Instead most of us choose to drain our energy and darken our powerful minds by looking at what others have chosen and criticizing their choices.

Just like a giant buffet there's plenty for everyone here. Just like a giant buffet every single person in line is going to make different choices about what they desire.

And believe it or not every single one of those choices is absolutely correct for the person who is making them *and no one else.*

To be blunt – what others choose is none of your business.

In life, as at the buffet, our choices are for ourselves. That is exactly how it should be.

Shouldn't we respect and celebrate the fact we all are different? We are so lucky to enjoy the freedom to choose exactly what we want at every moment. Why not give others the freedom to choose what brings them joy from the Buffet of Life without our interference?

I will end this book with my dream and deepest desire.

My dream is that as a race we will soon realize the profound truth of the Buffet of Life.

Then there will be no more lack, no more war, no more prejudice, no more hate.

No, all that will be left is a beautiful world of...

Unstoppable Joy!

THE SHAMAN

By Ed Osworth

This world is bad and folks make me mad
The things that I see are making me sad

Why am I a victim of all of this stuff?
Each direction I go is so awfully tough

I'll go to the Shaman, or maybe a Witch
Then I'll have someone to whom I can bitch

I'll ask her the future, then I'll know it all
No longer will I feel helpless and small

I went to The Shaman, her heart good as gold
She smiled and nodded. My story I told.

"Things in life will just not go my way
And I feel sick almost every day.

Other folks screw me all over the place,
And discourteous drivers get in my face.

I find that I'm angry all of the time
Cause others have stuff that should be mine

There's no one out there that's as good as me
So why do some have those great lives I see?

So tell me the future and open my eyes."
She said, "Do you want the truth or the lies?"

"The truth," I said, "no matter what."
Her look didn't kill, but deeply cut.

"The truth is your future will be just like now
Cause bad stuff you're seeing is all you allow

To enter your mind and settle in there
And grow in that brain that's under your hair

Like weeds in a garden you water with hate
The stuff that you're seeing is how you relate

To a beautiful world of wondrous sights
And the gift of a life of sweet delights

To gorgeous sunsets that make you cry
To the sweet smell of roses as you walk by

To the laughter of babies, the sight of first love
Spectacular clouds in the heavens above

To sun on your shoulders, wind in your hair
And delightful bird songs everywhere.

To wonderful people doing such good
Who bring food to the hungry in your neighborhood

This could be the world that catches your eyes
Instead of the world you claim you despise

The world inside you is what you will see
No other can change it, and that includes me

The world you see looks exactly like you
Angry and bitter, resentful and blue

You'll hate the future and all that you find
If you don't go to work and re train your mind

To be happy with now and enjoy every day
To focus on Joy, to laugh and to play

To leave all the hurts and the worries behind
And forgive all the insults that upset your mind

The future can't change things you're doing today
That form the tomorrows coming your way

To live in a kind world, simply be kind
Grab each and every chance that you find.

To help those in need or wearing a frown
Who could use a hand or are feeling down."

I couldn't believe all these things that she said
Those crazy ideas she put in my head

Like I was the cause of the trouble I see
It all comes from those not as good as me

My anger was rising and getting so hot
I told her right then she had better stop

The Shaman she paused, then her stare met my eye
"You asked for the truth, but you wanted the lie"

Her face turned quite sad, a tear formed a drop
I started to speak but that look made me stop

"Your future is bright, it will all come to you
Don't worry bout changing a thing that you do

Now thanks for your time, please be on your way
There are many truth seekers to see yet today."

Addendum

YOUR FREE BONUS AUDIOS

Visit our website and receive your free bonuses including audio downloads of me discussing and clarifying the concepts of "Unstoppable Joy." These are in MP3 audio format for your iPod, MP3 player or computer.

To download your bonuses simply visit the following link

http://unstoppablejoy.com/buyer

Our main website where you can visit us, download our free newsletter, find out about upcoming events and read more about *Unstoppable Joy* and The Joy Technique is:

http://UnstoppableJoy.com/

FREE GOOD NEWS

UNSTOPPABLE JOY NEWSLETTER

I invite you to join my **free newsletter**. It brings joy to you on a regular basis. It contains inspiring stories and good news as well as my unique opinions and musings.

You can subscribe to my newsletter three ways.

Send an email to

goodnews@unstoppablejoy.com

or go to

http://unstoppablejoy.com/subscribe

or fax your email address to **888-626-0454** with a note "add to newsletter"

ED'S FREE TELESEMINARS

Ed regularly schedules free teleseminars to chat with readers and answer questions regarding "Unstoppable Joy™" and "The Joy Technique™"

To see the schedule for upcoming free teleseminars simply visit:

http://UnstoppableJoy/teleseminar

UNSTOPPABLE JOY RESOURCES

We have a web page with links to many of the folks who are referred to in this book and others whose philosophies and businesses I respect and recommend at:

http://unstoppablejoy.com/resources

ED OSWORTH'S SPEAKING AND COACHING SERVICES

Ed is available for media interviews, speaking engagements, and corporate, personal and group training sessions.

Email Ed at:

ed@unstoppablejoy.com

or visit the website at:

http://UnstoppableJoy.com

and look for the link to "Ed's Services" for complete details

QUICK ORDER FORM

FAX orders to **888-626-0454**. Send this form or copy.
Email orders to **orders@unstoppablejoy.com**
Postal Orders: Oregon Dreams Publishing LLC,
PO Box 547, Lowell, OR 97452

Web Orders: Visit **http://UnstoppableJoy.com** and look for the order button.
Telephone Orders: Call **800-810-0998** toll free. Have your credit card ready.

Please send the following books, disks or reports. I understand that I may return them for a full refund – for any reason, no questions asked.

– –

– –

– –

– –

Please send me FREE information on:

Books_____Speaking____Coaching___Seminars _____

Name: _____

Address: _____

City: _____ State: ___ Zip: _____

Phone: _____

Fax:_____

Email Address: _____@_____

US Shipping: $4.00 for first book/disk and $2.00 each additional
International: $9.00 for first book/disk and $5.00 each additional